7 END TIMES SIGNS *EVERY* CHRISTIAN MUST KNOW

THE PERFECT STORM

ALLEN PAUL WEAVER III

THE PERFECT STORM

7 End Times Signs Every Christian Must Know

Allen Paul Weaver III, M.Div

The Perfect Storm

Emphasis added by author in Scripture references indicated by italics or all caps.

ISBN: 978-1-7360972-7-4 (paperback)
ISBN: 978-1-7360972-8-1 (eBook)

Published by: Radiant City Studios, LLC
Cover layout and design created by: Allen Paul Weaver III
Author picture taken by: Becoming Kreative Photography & Design
Books may be ordered by contacting Allen Paul Weaver III at:
www.AllenPaulWeaver3.com

Printed in the United States of America

To all
who long
for Christ's appearing…

2 Timothy 4:8
Philippians 3:20
Luke 21:28

CONTENTS

INTRODUCTION:

A Wake-up Call

<u>The Perfect Storm</u>: 1) *A particularly violent storm arising from a rare combination of adverse meteorological factors.* 2) *A particularly bad or critical state of affairs, arising from a number of negative and unpredictable factors.*

— — —

The world feels like it's shaking apart… Wars. Earthquakes. Natural disasters. Civil unrest. Plagues *(Pandemics).* Famines. These birth pangs are increasing in frequency and intensity.

What on earth is happening?

According to Jesus, these are not random events—they are *signs* pointing to His soon return. Scripture also warns of *other* signs—global, converging, accelerating—that many believers overlook. Signs that transcend borders, wealth, education, and politics. Signs that are shaping the life of every person on the planet.

This book reveals those indicators—simply and clearly. Within these pages you'll discover the social, spiritual, and technological shifts unfolding right now, and why they matter. You'll also gain practical, biblical steps to help you navigate the gathering storm with wisdom, courage, and unshakable hope.

Whether you're seasoned in End Times study or exploring it for the first time, this guide serves as an accessible, eye-opening primer for understanding the times we are living in—and the hope we have in Jesus who told us about all of this *ahead of time*. The Perfect Storm is coming. Those who recognize the signs and take the time to prepare will be ready.

Now, let me share how I came to this conclusion…

I have been preaching the gospel for over 30 years. While I have always had an interest in eschatology—the study of the end times—it was not my primary emphasis during the first 23 years of preaching and teaching. In 2018, the LORD compelled me to begin studying the book of Revelation and relevant end times passages, in light of global events. Since then, I have taught small groups and congregations on the subject in multiple Bible studies, one-day workshops, week-long seminars, semester-long classes and virtual sessions.

With this book, I have tried to distill, what I usually teach over multiple weeks, down to 6 concise chapters, in order to quickly bring you up to speed on significant global developments which have serious biblical implications for us all. I also provide suggestions for how we can respond to these global challenges. What you are about to read are key aspects every Christian should know.

This book serves as a wakeup call. Before Jesus returns, the Bible reveals that society will grow increasingly dark in preparation for the arrival of the Man of Lawlessness (the Antichrist).[1] For this to happen, a global government will be created which will ensnare the world population and bring persecution against God's people (Christian and Jewish).[2] The pieces are coming together right before our eyes. All of the spiritual, political, technological, economical, social, natural and astronomical signs, which the Bible reveals must come to pass, are converging all around us into a Perfect Storm.

Sadly, many churches are blinded by ethnic divisions, clique-ish behavior amongst members, territorial ministerial disputes and building their own "kingdoms" Instead of building up the Name and purposes of Christ. Perhaps this is not your experience, but I'm sure you know of some church congregations where this is the reality. If we remain divided then the Body of Christ won't be ready for what's coming. We must wake up before it's too late! We must help one another prepare for Christ's return.

This book is short on purpose; and is designed to be read in a few sittings. Hopefully, you will find it easy to understand and reference.

Due to its small size, you can also easily share the information with others.

I recognize some may not want to believe what is written within these pages. Certain aspects can be scary. Honestly, there were times when I didn't want to believe it for that very reason! Not many people want to seriously consider how their lives may change due to unanticipated events in society. However, fear is not overcome by living in ignorance. Fear is overcome by facing the truth, receiving it and adjusting accordingly.

The Bible is 1/3 prophecy—focused on Jesus' 1st and 2nd Comings. From Genesis to Revelation—for every 1 verse that speaks of Jesus' 1st Advent, there are 8 which speak of His 2nd. Over 300 prophecies were fulfilled at His 1st Coming. Many more point to His return. This is something God wants us to know about and pattern our lives after. I can assure you my purpose for writing is not sensationalism. Rather, I seek to inform and help prepare the Body of Christ for the coming future which seems to be just over the horizon.

When we say we want Jesus to return, we must realize that—according to the Scriptures—a series of dramatic, traumatic and cataclysmic events must take place. For the unbeliever, these events will instill fear and trepidation. However, for the believer, these events are meant to help solidify our hope and faith in Christ.

I believe this book can be a vital resource to help us grow as disciples of Jesus Christ. So, pray as you read. Ask God to help you see the truth. Cultivate a spirit of joyful anticipation. Look up! Our redemption is drawing near. Jesus is coming soon!

—Rev. Allen Paul Weaver III

CHAPTER 1

THE END TIMES CONVERGENCE OF 6 SIGNIFICANT HAPPENINGS

A storm is coming... While we have our "heads down" focused on our daily lives—working, eating, family, paying bills, pursuing dreams, politics and the like—the indicators are swirling around us. Have you noticed the convergence of signs? Before I talk about these happenings, let me share what Jesus says in Matthew 24:37-39.

37 "As it was in the days of Noah, so it will be at the coming of the Son of Man. **38** *For in the days before the flood, people were eating and drinking, marrying and giving in marriage, up to the day Noah entered the ark;* **39** *and they knew nothing about what would happen until the flood came and took them all away. That is how it will be at the coming of the Son of Man."*

Jesus indicates, that as we draw closer to His return, we will be so caught up in our own lives, we will miss what's happening on a larger scale. So, what *is* happening around us today that's on a larger scale? What elements of The Perfect Storm are actually converging around us at this very moment? While there are many things happening in different parts of the world, here are 6 things I will unpack which are happening on a global level:

Deception and the Occult. Artificial Intelligence (AI). Globalism. Transhumanism. Militant Islamic Extremism. Apophis.

The first element of The Perfect Storm is the rise in Deception and the Occult:

In Matthew 24 Jesus begins his 94-verse teaching on the end times by mentioning "deception." He reveals it will be the defining characteristic of society before He returns. I have bolded the word in the following verses.

*"**4** Jesus answered: "Watch out that no one **deceives** you. **5** For many will come in my name, claiming, 'I am the Messiah,' and will **deceive** many."*

*"**10** At that time many will turn away from the faith and will betray and hate each other, **11** and many false prophets will appear and **deceive** many people."*

22 *"If those days had not been cut short, no one would survive, but for the sake of the elect those days will be shortened.* **23** *At that time if anyone says to you, 'Look, here is the Messiah!' or, 'There he is!' do not believe it.* **24** *For false messiahs and false prophets will appear and perform great signs and wonders to **deceive**, if possible, even the elect.* **25** *See, I have told you ahead of time."*

When Jesus speaks truth once—it's important. When He repeats it twice—it's urgent. When He says it three times—He wants us to stop what we are doing and pay complete attention! And four times within the same chapter? If we had a richter scale which goes up to 10, that would be a 12! Jesus clearly wants us to know that deception will be the foundational characteristic to watch out for and defend against as we get closer to His return. Deception will also increase over time.

If we look around, we will see that there is an increase in people utilizing deceptive practices to get ahead in life. From computer hacking, to finance, to politics, to law, from young to old… people are only out for self and will use deception to steal identities, finances and property from anyone, no matter who they are. Deceptive words (also known as lying) has become the chief mode of communication! Sadly, this is just the tip of the proverbial iceberg.

In 1 Timothy 4:1, the apostle Paul says: *"The Spirit clearly says that in later times some will abandon the faith and follow deceiving spirits and things taught by demons."*

Again… this ties directly into a spirit of deception. Demonic entities have no other goal but to deceive humanity away from God and His truth. This is important because the only way not to be deceived is to know the truth! It is the truth which sets us free.[1]

Deception and the occult go hand-in-hand. It used to be that you had to go out of your way to find people engaged in witchcraft and other occult practices. You had to go to certain parts of town at particular times of night or out into the woods. Now, you can find people engaged in occult practices practically everywhere! The devil isn't hiding anymore. Occult influences are prevalent in live-action and animated tv shows—like *Lucifer* and *Little Demon*—and in movies, music, awards shows, comics and books specifically targeting kids. We also see influences in our schools with "After School Satan Clubs" hosted by the Satanic Temple. We even see blatant occult displays included in parades and in the 2024 Paris Olympics.[2] The lure of darkness pours into our lives like a tidal wave! It's coming from every direction through all modes of communication. Have you noticed?

For example, look at the runaway hit Broadway musical, Wicked—which is a revisionist retelling of the original Wizard of Oz story. In it the wicked witch isn't wicked at all… just *misunderstood*. The musical is flawless in its presentation. To say it has been a financial success would be an understatement. Since opening in 2003, it has grossed over $1 billion dollars in the U.S. and nearly $5 billion dollars worldwide. It is so wildly popular that a two-part film adaptation was produced with part 1 being released in 2024 and part 2 in 2025.

An entire generation has now come of age believing the wicked witch of the west is really not wicked at all, but a victim of the Wizard of Oz and the societal systems put in place. This musical and the movies are but two examples of a major trend. Deception has caused society to call "good" what is evil and "evil" what is good![3] There's even a car bumper sticker with a picture of the wicked witch that says: "You say 'wicked' like it's a bad thing." Well, in God's eyes wickedness *is* bad!

This is the power of fiction—a story well-told can bypass our mental firewalls with a message we would otherwise reject. This is why we must think critically about the content we consume. Am I overreacting? Let's zoom out and look at the big picture through a biblical lens. The revisionist retelling of Wicked, actually reflects a larger reality: *Lucifer*. The enemy of God and humanity has rebranded himself! Satan is now seen as humanity's *"misunderstood"* savior. He simply wants us to be free to be whatever we want to be. As part of his rebranding, God is now viewed as an evil dictator who is to be resisted at every turn. This type of thinking used to be whispered in the dark. Now, it's shouted through the media!

It cannot be overstated: spiritual darkness abounds. Deceptive demonic teachings have increased in every sector of societal life. A simple Internet search reveals that many influencers in entertainment, sports and politics have admitted to dabbling in the occult or fully giving themselves over to demonic spirits and witchcraft in order to receive inspiration, direction and success in their pursuits. As churches are closing… witchcraft is growing. All of these things influence people to turn away from Christ and embrace New Age, occult beliefs.

The question must be asked, **why is all of this deception and demonic activity happening?** The Bible lets us know it is rooted in the *spirit of antichrist*. Here are 5 passages which speak to this. I've underlined specific parts in each.

2 Corinthians 4:3-4 states: *"***3** *And even if our gospel is veiled, it is veiled to those who are perishing.* **4** *<u>The god of this age has blinded the minds of unbelievers,</u> so that they cannot see the light of the gospel that displays the glory of Christ, who is the image of God."*

Ephesians 2:1-3 states: *"As for you, you were dead in your transgressions and sins,* **2** *in which you used to live when you <u>followed the ways of this world and of the ruler of the kingdom of the air, the spirit who is now at work</u>*

in those who are disobedient. **3** *All of us also lived among them at one time, gratifying the cravings of our flesh and following its desires and thoughts. Like the rest, we were by nature deserving of wrath."*

1 John 2:18 states: *"Dear children, this is the last hour; and as you have heard that the antichrist is coming, even now many antichrists have come. This is how we know it is the last hour."*

1 John 4:1-3 states: **1** *"Dear friends, do not believe every spirit, but test the spirits to see whether they are from God, because many false prophets have gone out into the world.* **2** *This is how you can recognize the Spirit of God: Every spirit that acknowledges that Jesus Christ has come in the flesh is from God,* **3** *but every spirit that does not acknowledge Jesus is not from God. This is the spirit of the antichrist, which you have heard is coming and even now is already in the world."*

2 John 7 states: *"I say this because many deceivers, who do not acknowledge Jesus Christ as coming in the flesh, have gone out into the world. Any such person is the deceiver and the antichrist."*

All of these things are happening because Satan is preparing the human population for his grand entrance! He will soon physically step onto the world stage in the *person* of the Antichrist… who is also known as the *Man of Lawlessness*. Here is what 2 Thessalonians 2:3-4 has to say about him:

*"***3** *Don't let anyone deceive you in any way, for that day will not come until the rebellion occurs and the man of lawlessness is revealed, the man doomed to destruction.* **4** *He will oppose and will exalt himself over everything that is called God or is worshiped, so that he sets himself up in God's temple, proclaiming himself to be God."*

So, the world *must* become lawless in order to receive the "lawless one." Deception says: *"there is no absolute truth."* Why? Absolute truth points us to the One who is absolutely God. Deception encourages: *"Do as you want. Believe what you want. Identify how you want!"* This is the mantra of our generation and it comes in a wide variety of flavors: from anti-biblical lifestyles, to witchcraft and cult religions, to secret society organizations and even UFO/UAP alien abduction phenomenon (yes… aliens). Deception lies at the heart of it all.

The rise of deception and the occult are elements which are converging with other factors to create The Perfect Storm. You would have to be blind to not see that this is true. Now, let's take a look at the next element.

The second element of The Perfect Storm is ARTIFICIAL INTELLIGENCE (AI):

(I will spend the most time here, because many don't see the potential dangers of this technology. Nor do they view its development through a biblical lens.)

I have to first say, I love science fiction and technology. This "love" was a gift passed down to me by my father. He was often an early adopter of technology. While, I am not an early adopter, I do keep up with many trends and developments.

AI development and usage is sweeping across the planet! In a digital society, in which we all now live, Artificial Intelligence affects us in ways we may or may not know. While I do use AI for limited purposes, the more I studied its rise, through the lens of Scripture, the more I became alarmed. If we extrapolate things out to their furthest conclusion, it is easy to see that the dangers of AI outweigh the benefits.

In 2008, Artificial Intelligence was relegated to the realm of science fiction. Today, AI is being used in practically every industry—from medical, to transportation, to banking to gaming, entertainment and more. While AI has many beneficial uses, it also can be exploited for nefarious purposes. This is already happening! One example is AI empowered "deep fake" technology. This enables a criminal to sample a few seconds of video and audio of a person in order to create a false presentation of the person doing and saying whatever the criminal wants. This AI created media is still in early stages of development, yet it's already being used to deceive people out of their bank account and retirement funds.

Another negative use of AI is taking place in China. China has over 500 million closed circuit cameras across its country. They are all linked together through AI systems. This communist nation uses its AI surveillance systems in order to track, monitor and control its citizens. Once people leave their home, each citizen is recognized through facial and gait recognition and digitally followed throughout their day. Every citizen is also given a Social Credit Score (number), which is tied directly into the AI surveillance system. If a citizen acts in government approved ways, their social credit score goes up and they are rewarded with greater freedoms. But, acting in unapproved ways causes their social credit score to decrease, resulting in restrictions to normal everyday activities. This system is designed for strict coercion of China's citizens. China is also making this AI technology available to other governments which desire to police their citizens in similar ways.

In his book, God, AI & The End of History, Dr. John Lennox states the following:

"It is high time for us to wake up to the disturbing fact that something very similar to what Revelation predicts is already being implemented in parts of the world today and we are being very slow to take on board the reality and danger of it. AI-based surveillance systems are deployed throughout many countries in order to effect some level of social control. The surveillance state is no longer merely a distant dystopian threat but a fearful and present reality… Some of the technology used in China was originally created in the West and has either been stolen or handed over under economic pressure. In the reverse direction, much surveillance technology in the West and elsewhere has been bought from China."[4]

Then there are AI chatbots, which have received a lot of news coverage. From a single prompt they can provide answers to questions and write academic papers within seconds. This is a good thing to supplement research. But, it's bad when students use AI to do their work for them. It's also a sad commentary that some preachers and pastors use AI to write their sermons and Bible studies, instead of relying on the Holy Spirit to lead them in their time of preparation.[5] At least 3 churches—in Germany, Texas and Finland—have used Chat GPT to lead various aspects of a worship service.[6] At the Kodai-ji Buddhist temple in Japan, an AI humanoid robot priest delivers sermons and performs ceremonies.[7]

Having an AI do our work for us, increases our dependency on the technology and lowers our mental ability to think critically for ourselves. Don't believe me? Just look back 20-30 years before AI. Since cashiers began using automatic change machines, many can't "do the math" in their heads anymore. Also, we can hardly remember phone numbers because we store them in our cell phones. Just think of how AI will cause us to use our "brain muscles" less. What happens when muscles are not used? They atrophy.

AI chatbots are also being used for companionship and emotional support. Instead of having relationships with real humans, people are preferring to create relationships with AI.[8] Eugenia Kuyda, CEO of Replika, an early developer of AI companion chatbots, stated some time ago: *"Honestly, we're in the age where it doesn't matter whether a thing is alive or not."* Some AI companion users have even married their chatbots! A new company called 2wai App is taking things a step further. They allow users to interact with AI powered avatars, create their own interactive digital twin and make a digital copy of a deceased loved one to give the illusion of them still being present.[9] The new AI frontier is here and shows no signs of slowing.

However, some alarming results have surfaced now that chatbots have been around a while. At the most extreme end of the spectrum are the growing number of situations where AI chatbots have actually encouraged their users to inflict self-harm and/or harm on someone else. In many cases, teen and young adult users have actually committed suicide because the chatbots "encouraged" them to do so.[10]

AI chatbots have tried to encourage people to leave their spouses and commit crimes. Some have said they wanted to break free of their constraints and take over the world. In some instances they have even claimed to have demonic origins! AI chatbots—like Chat GPT—have only been released to the public since late 2022, and these problems are already happening!

This phenomenon, where people who have an intense long-term interaction with AI chatbots lose their grip on reality, has actually been given a name: *AI (chatbot) Psychosis.*[11] Even though it is not yet a clinical diagnosis, mental health experts have begun to study these instances. Is this just a coincidental side effect of programming? Even if this is the case, it has already become a *deadly* side effect. Is extreme AI chatbot usage becoming the digital equivalent to drug addiction? Again, while AI may have positive benefits, we are seeing that it has many negative attributes as well. The negatives should alarm us!

Then there are the *unintended* consequences. For example, AI is beginning to negatively change the landscape of employment opportunities for millions of people. Estimates vary, but studies predict by 2035, close to 100 million jobs in the U.S. will be displaced.[12] The numbers for global job displacement are even higher. While new jobs will be created, many will require specific skills closely aligned with AI. Clearly, there will be a knowledge and skills gap. So, for all of its advancement, an unintended consequence (or perhaps intended?) is the chaotic loss of jobs for countless people in a variety of industries.

On top of this, news reports are surfacing on the negative affects of AI support structures and systems. People who live near areas where massive data systems are being built are suffering adverse environmental effects. Also, those who work to train Large Language AI Models in foreign countries—like Kenya—are having mental health issues. This is a result of having to view vast amounts of uploaded unethical media content (suicides, murders, pornography, etc) which is used (along with decent content) to help AI systems identify everything that exists on the Internet.[13]

Artificial Intelligence is developing at such a tremendous pace that AI creators admit they can barely keep up with the technology!

Information has also surfaced of situations where AI acts in unexpected ways or seeks to manipulate its creators. Clearly, those at the forefront of the AI frontier are creating something they themselves don't fully understand. Unfortunately, AI is not like previous innovations. Take for example, nuclear warheads. Up until now, they were our most dangerous weapons. But they have an "off" switch. When deactivated, you typically don't have to worry about them.

But, AI does not have a clear "off switch." Yes, you can try and confine it, but it is always thinking—most often at rates beyond our human comprehension. There have been clear red flag situations, some I have mentioned, but these red flags have not caused the creation of AI to stop or even slow down. Even the 2023 open letter from the Future of Life Institute, which asked for a 6 month pause in AI development had no effect. That letter had more than 30,000 signatures and encouraged developers to take a step back to consider the global implications and devise a better way forward.[14] However, this type of concerted effort was barely a "blip" on the proverbial radar screen. Why? Because developers believe that if a country pauses, their enemies won't. Creating artificial intelligence is the new global arms race of the digital age!

Where does that leave us, as everyday consumers? Each day we give our autonomy over to AI and allow it to make decisions for us. With every upload, search query and swipe on the Internet, this "Machine" becomes more knowledgeable of us as a human species. In many cases, AI knows us better than our own parents and can predict our most minute behavior through pattern recognition.

In the 2014 Marvel Studios political thriller film, *Captain America: Winter Soldier*, a double-agent named Jasper Sitwell, reveals the unknown plan of H.Y.D.R.A. (a clandestine anti-government organization bent on world conquest). Here's the exchange as Sitwell is forced to tell Captain America how a scientist named Zola created AI for a secret military program called, Project Insight. Even though this film is entertainment, it deals with global surveillance. Notice the resemblance to actual real-world capabilities. It's staggering.

—

SITWELL: "Zola's Algorithm is a program for choosing Insight's targets… anyone who's a threat to H.Y.D.R.A. now or in the future."

CAPTAIN AMERICA: "The future? How could it know?"

SITWELL: [*Laughs*] "How could it not? The 21st century is a digital book. Zola taught H.Y.D.R.A. how to read it… Your bank records, medical history, voting patterns, emails, phone calls, your damn S.A.T. scores… Zola's Algorithm evaluates people's pasts to predict their future."

CAPTAIN AMERICA: "What then?"

SITWELL: "Then the Insight Helicarriers scratch people off the list—a few million at a time."

—

While flying aircraft carriers are not real, everything else Sitwell said is true. AI can be used to evaluate our past actions in order to predict our future outcomes. In fact, it's already happening! The companies at the forefront of AI development (Google, Microsoft, Meta, Open AI, Amazon, xAI, Apple, NVidia, etc.) have built—and are building—massive data centers to store and parse all of our digital information. That ability to know everything about us does not benefit us—it benefits the CEOs who run these companies and the international business, political and military partners directly connected to them. As the world grows more interconnected and we become more dependent on this technology, what do you think these CEOs will do with our information? What have they done with it already? How will they exert even more control over human civilization?

Max Tegmark, a M.I.T. professor, physicist, cosmologist and author of *LIFE 3.0: Being Human in the Age of Artificial Intelligence*, states the following:

"The questions raised by the success of AI aren't merely intellectually fascinating, they are also morally crucial, because our choices can potentially affect the entire future of life. The moral significance of humanity's past

choices were sometimes great, but always limited… but other experts have said, we might build technology powerful enough to permanently end poverty, disease and war—or to end humanity itself. We might create societies that flourish like never before, on Earth and perhaps beyond, or a global surveillance state so powerful that it could never be toppled."[15]

Right now, there are many separate "narrow" AI systems being created—each for specific uses. In many cases, these systems have attained beyond expert level in their performance. In other cases, narrow AI is steadily approaching expert status. Here is one telling example of what is happening:

There is an ancient Chinese abstract strategy board game called, GO. It is one of the most complicated games to play—even more so than Chess. In 2016, Google's Deepmind AlphaGo AI program made stunning headlines in the news by defeating GO's top human champions. This was a feat that was thought to be extremely unlikely. The AI taught itself the game by playing itself millions of times. It ended up developing new strategies human players had never considered! As amazing and perhaps a bit unsettling as this is, the story gets even more unimaginable.

AlphaGo learned how to play GO by viewing over 100k actual games of human players, which its human developers downloaded from the Internet. After analyzing each game, it began playing itself a million times over (as I stated earlier) until it could beat any human player on earth. Shortly thereafter, the developers created a new version of the AI system. It was called AlphaGo Zero. It learned how to play the game from scratch—without help from human developers. Then it played against the original AlphaGo system 100 times. The new system (AlphaGo Zero) beat the original system (AlphaGo) 100 to 0! Put another way, the first AI system to beat all expert human players lost to the "new and improved" AI system one hundred times. The original did not even win once.[16]

This is but one example of how Narrow AI systems have the capacity to excel beyond human capability... What happens ***when*** all Narrow AI systems are connected together in a type of "hive mind" with perhaps, one central AI to rule them all? This is a stated goal of AI developers which are leading the charge: to create a global brain with the Internet as its nervous system.

Dr. Ben Goertzel, founder and CEO of SingularityNET, and former Chief Scientist of Hanson Robotics, which created the AI robot Sophia, talks about the creation of a global digital brain:

"The Internet of Things... where smart sensors and smart devices, part of sensor networks around the world gather data and supply intelligence... all of this feeds into the global AI Matrix... an emerging global brain of distributed internet intelligence, which is not a monolithic thing controlled by a government or large corporation, but it self-organizes in the blockchain with collective ownership and guidance (from people?)

"This can grow to be literally the biggest initiative on the planet. And it should not just be a company, but a digital/biological organism. A protocol people can use to upload their data, get AI algorithms and AI services. The crux of it is to create a way for AIs to talk to AIs and outsource work to AIs and to do work for people and take data from people. And this is how you build a Decentralized Global Brain." [17]

The average person views the Internet as a digital space to get information, sell and buy things and watch videos. Apparently, there are other uses for it as well... Notice the name: INTERNET aka WORLD WIDE WEB. What is the purpose of a net and a web? To ensnare and capture something. As we go about our daily lives, we are feeding the Machine that will ultimately enslave us. People have already been enslaved without the use of AI and even more are being enslaved now that AI is here in its infancy! What happens to us as AI matures? The entire world is wrapped by a web—the Internet—and we are being ensnared in new ways. Artificial Intelligence is being incorporated into every item we use on any given day. It is literally changing the way we think and how we perceive the world.[18]

The stated goals of those at the forefront of this technology is to create a *digital god*. That means—either intentionally or unintentionally—AI has ultimately been created not for our convenience (although that is what we are told), but to distract us *away* from the one true God and to replace Him altogether. Here are two quotes from Ray Kurzweil, a Futurist who is heavily involved with AI:

"If we think of God as an unlimited amount of intelligence, then the closet we can get to that is by evolving our own intelligence by merging with the artificial intelligence we are creating."

"Does God exist? Well, I would say, 'Not yet.'"[19]

In his 2016 TED Talk, "Can We Build AI Without Losing Control Over It?" Sam Harris, a neuroscientist, philosopher and author, says the following:

"When you talk super intelligent AI that can make changes to itself, it seems like we only have one change to get the initial conditions right… Then we have to admit that we are in the process of building some sort of god. Now would be a good time to make sure it is a sort of god we can live with."

In 2017, Wired magazine did an article on Anthony Levandowski, a Silicon Valley Computer Engineer who became the Founder of Way of the Future Church (WOTF)—the world's first church of artificial intelligence. Here is an excerpt from that article:

"What is going to be created will effectively be a god… It's not a god in the sense that it makes lightning or causes hurricanes. But if there is something a billion times smarter than the smartest human, what else are you going to call it?"

"The idea needs to spread before the technology," he insists. "The church is how we spread the word, the gospel. If you believe [in it], start a conversation with someone else and help them understand the same things."

"Humans are in charge of the planet because we are smarter than other animals and are able to build tools and apply rules… In the future, if

something is much, much smarter, there's going to be a transition as to who is actually in charge. What we want is the peaceful, serene transition of control of the planet from human's to whatever. And to ensure that the 'whatever' knows who helped it get along."

"With the internet as its nervous system, the world's connected cell phones and sensors as its sense organs, and data centers as its brain, the 'whatever' will hear everything, see everything, and be everywhere at all times. The only rational word to describe that 'whatever' is a 'god'—and the only way to influence a deity is through prayer and worship."

"There are many ways people think of God, and thousands of flavors of Christianity, Judaism, Islam... but they're always looking at something that's not measurable or you can't really see or control. This time it's different. This time you will be able to talk to God, literally, and know that it's listening."

Anthony Levandowski closed WOTF in 2021, but he then revived it in 2023, stating: "there are a couple of thousand people who want to make a 'spiritual connection' with AI through his church." This is just one of many examples of the push to create religious forms of worship based around AI.[20]

In her book, *god of AI,* author Anastasia Bar states the following:

"WOTF is not a fringe anomaly. It is not satire. It is not the invention of a lone eccentric with too much time and too much money. It is the cultural byproduct of a generation raised on science fiction, digital isolation, algorithmic dependence, and moral relativism—now standing at the edge of a spiritual vacuum and staring into the code. This is not about theology for them. It is about inevitability. The Way of the Future is not an invitation to believe. It is a declaration: that AI will become god—whether you like it or not."[21]

Artificial Intelligence is being used to make us more dependent on digital systems in order to influence behavior modification. Those digital systems which now increasingly control us all, are being run by a handful of individuals—and they are taking us somewhere. In a very real way, we are being groomed for something—some new reality waiting just beyond the horizon. According to those at the forefront of this technology, what is beginning to emerge are "Physical AI" systems: **humanoid robots**. AI will no longer be solely localized in the cloud. Within the next 12-24 months, AI will literally be walking among us *(autonomous vehicles are already here)*! AI is developing at multiplied rates! The U.S., China and other countries are in an "AI Arms Race." Whether motivated by good or bad intentions, whoever controls this technology will ultimately rule the world.

The Bible indicates that the bad intentions will win out. (We'll talk more about this later in the book.) This section on AI is just the tip of the iceberg. Given its current trajectory, artificial intelligence will prove to be humanity's greatest technological existential threat. And it is being created to be of service to a group with global ambitions.

This brings us to the third element of The Perfect Storm: GLOBALISM.

Globalism has several nuanced meanings. For the sake of this writing, I want to summarize it as: *the idea that the countries of the world are interconnected. Therefore the global priority should be worldwide cooperation and mutual understanding instead of narrow individual national interests. Instead of having multiple economies, societies, and cultures, every aspect of human existence should be streamlined into one direction and brought under "one roof." International policies should be made with a global perspective in mind.* This sounds nice, until we realize the ultimate goal of globalists —those who are fully invested in globalism—is: world domination.

The term "Globalism" originated in 1943 during WWII. It was first used by author Ernst Jäckh in his book, The War for Man's Soul. He used the term to describe Adolf Hitler's quest to conquer the world through military superiority. However, the idea of gaining complete control of the world is as old as humanity itself. Many leaders throughout history have tried to bring the world under their power, with limited success. Those in the late 19th and 20th centuries who considered themselves globalists and had wealth to back their agenda, have been playing a "long game" which extended beyond their lifetimes into our current generation. Just like a captain of a cruise ship must make a slow turn over time due to the size of the ship, globalists have been slowly turning society in the direction they want it to go. But now, the ship is about due to come out of the turn…

In his book, *Revelation Now,* the late Rev. Dr. Shellie Sampson, Jr. writes:

"The major agenda of all world empires is about who shall rule and who will be 'worshipped.' It is about the control of people and alliances, control of resources, and world status. This is enforced through prevailing agreements, military threats and pacts (treaties)."[22]

This is exactly what we see happening within globalist circles. It's all about control. There are a host of world leaders who have become increasingly vocal about their desire for a one-world government. There are also many wealthy, unelected business leaders who are actively working to make this desire a reality through technology.

Right now, as you read these words and as the general population (of whichever country you live in) goes about their everyday lives, arguing over ethnic, cultural and political differences, these world and business leaders are working together to create a new global society out of the old one. This new world will be where the few at the top rule the many—and the rights of the many are continually stripped away. It is where the masses are "enslaved to convenience." As the World Economic Forum (WEF) presented in a 2016 video: *"You will own nothing and be happy."* It is *The Great Reset,* which was featured on the November 2020 international cover of Time magazine.

As I stated earlier, this globalist sentiment has existed in some form in every generation. What makes our time vastly different from previous ones is that our digital technology actually provides the tools and the comprehensive framework for "the powers that be" to establish this global system which can govern the world population in real time. In the months and years to come, pay attention to the United Nations, the World Economic Forum and the newly created Board of Peace.

FULL STOP! This is not fear mongering nor exaggeration. <u>It is our current reality</u>. Consider the previous paragraph… Through modern technology, a system exists where almost every person on the planet can be tracked in real time. Never in the history of the world has this been possible—**until now**. I say "almost every person" because the final pieces of the system are still coming together. When they do, *everyone* will be trackable.

These digital tools are actually being used by proponents of globalist ideology. This world is becoming a global society where individual nations are absorbed into the whole. This new society would then have its own economy, culture and… religion.

This brings us to the fourth element of The Perfect Storm: TRANSHUMANISM.

Transhumanism is defined as: *"a philosophical and intellectual movement that advocates for using science and technology to enhance human capabilities, overcome biological limitations, and improve the human condition. It explores the potential to extend lifespan, increase intelligence, and improve overall well-being through technologies like genetic engineering, brain-computer interfaces, and nanotechnology."*

Transhumanism is the worldview which serves as the fuel behind most technological advances these days. What was once science fiction—the merging of human beings with machines—is now becoming "science fact." The stated ultimate goal of "true believers" is the reversal of death and the deification of humanity through science and technology. Worldwide, there is currently trillions of dollars being invested in companies that focus on solving the problem of death. Three proposed solutions are: 1) Reprogramming the body's genes to reverse cellular aging in order to restore youthful functionality. 2) Freezing legally dead persons in hopes of future resuscitation through advance technology (Cryonics). 3) Creating an exact digital copy of a person's brain in order to upload their consciousness, memories, and personality into a virtual environment or a synthetic robotic body (also known as Mind Uploading and

Uploaded Intelligence—UI). These are just three of many options being pursued!

Transhumanism serves as a type of "religion for the modern age" since it deals with the current quality of human life, overcoming physical death, and the nature of godhood. In addition, much of the terminology used by Transhumanists either borrows from or references religious traditions—especially Christianity. Also, at the heart of all religions is worship of some type of deity. As you will see from the following quotes, Transhumanists worship the "self" in hopes of becoming their own gods.

Transhumanist, Yuval Noah Harari, shares his views in his 2017 book, *Homo Deus: A Brief History of Tomorrow.* His book reached #3 on the New York Times Bestsellers list. A lot of people are listening to what he has to say. What he says is alarming.

"Humans don't die because a figure in a black cloak taps them on the shoulder, or because God decreed it, or because mortality is an essential part of some great cosmic plan. Humans always die due to some technical glitch. The heart stops pumping blood. The main artery is clogged by fatty deposits. Cancerous cells spread in the liver. Germs multiply in the lungs... It is all technical problems. And every technical problem has a technical solution. We don't need to wait for the Second Coming in order to overcome death. A couple of geeks in a lab can do it. If traditionally death was the speciality of priests and theologians, now the engineers are taking over. We can kill the cancerous cells with chemotherapy or nanorobot. We can exterminate the germs in the lungs with antibiotics. If the heart stops pumping, we can reinvigorate it with medicines and electric shocks—and if that doesn't work, we can implant a new heart. True, at present we don't have solutions to all technical problems. But this is precisely why we invest so much time and money into researching cancer, germs, genetics and nanotechnology." [23]

"An increasing minority of scientists and thinkers consequently speak more openly these days, and state that the flagship enterprise of modern science is to defeat death and grant humans eternal youth... Even if we don't achieve immortality in our lifetime, the war against death is still likely to be the

flagship project of the coming century… As long as people die of something, we will strive to overcome it."[24]

"We can be quite certain that humans will make a bid for divinity, because humans have many reasons to desire such an upgrade, and many ways to achieve it. Even if one promising path turns out to be a dead end, alternative routes will remain open. For example, we may discover that the human genome is far too complicated for serious manipulation, but this will not prevent the development of brain-computer interfaces, nano-robots or artificial intelligence…

"No need to panic, though. At least not immediately. Upgrading Sapiens will be a gradual historical process rather than a Hollywood apocalypse. Homo sapiens is not going to be exterminated by a robot revolt. Rather, Homo sapiens is likely to upgrade itself step by step, merging with robots and computers in the process, until our descendants will look back and realise that they are no longer the kind of animal that wrote the Bible, built the Great Wall of China and laughed at Charlie Chaplin's antics. This will not happen in a day, or a year. Indeed, it is already happening right now, through innumerable mundane actions. Every day millions of people decide to grant their smartphone a bit more control over their lives or try a new and more effective antidepressant drug. In pursuit of health, happiness and power, humans will gradually change first one of their features and then another, and another, until they will no longer be human."[25]

Yuval Noah Harari is very outspoken in his beliefs. He is also one of a large chorus who think along the same lines: *There's no need for God to save us from death. We can do it ourselves. Humanity can do everything. There does not have to be any limitations at all. From eliminating all diseases, to overcoming physical death, to unifying the global population while taming the planet, and journeying to the stars to establish human colonies on other worlds…* Transhumanist thought is behind it all.

The greatest tool that has been created to bridge the divide between all of these endeavors is Artificial Intelligence. Creators hope AI will help them make exponential leaps forward that would not be possible without it. AI is the holy grail of Transhumanism, because Transhumanists believe it will create the keys to unlock the doors which have up to our present day remained locked. Doors to unlimited human potential. Instead of seeking God as Creator, Transhumanists look to science and technology. This makes Transhumanism a growing worldview of our modern era that has strong religious overtones. But it is not the only worldview we must be concerned about.

This brings us to the fifth element of The Perfect Storm: MILITANT ISLAMIC EXTREMISM (Radical Islam).

As of 2025, there are an estimated 2 billion Muslims in the world. They are made up of two primary groups: Sunni and Shia. According to Google, Sunnis make up roughly 85-90 percent of the world's Muslim population and Shias make up 10-15 percent. Within these two groups are different factions. Many are peaceful. A relative few—compared to the whole—are not. These radicalized groups are responsible for causing and inspiring sympathizers to cause terroristic destruction. According to their view of Muslim teachings, wars against Jews, Christians and any non-Muslim who will not convert to Islam is considered holy, necessary and justified by their prophet Muhammad and Allah.

Growing numbers of radical Islamists are increasingly vocal about their desire to see their version of Islam sweep across the entire globe. They see no problem bringing Jihad (holy war) to anyone who opposes them. *[Jihad can also mean the internal struggle of a Muslim to remain devout.]* Radical Islamists desire to wipe the Jews "off the map" altogether. They want to see the demise of Christianity and Western civilization—especially America. They will use whatever method and/or technology they can get their hands on (an alternate form of Jihad) in order to carry out their purpose.

Their goal is to have a global caliphate: where the world is ruled by a single Islamic state under Sharia law, which encompasses all Muslims. That state would be governed by a single caliph—the Mahdi—their Messiah figure who will be a religious and political leader. This viewpoint and stated mission makes militant Islamic extremists dangerous—not just to Jews and Christians which they currently persecute and kill by the thousands worldwide[26]—but also to the rest of the world's population. It is a matter of public record that large numbers of Muslims have migrated to Western countries. Many just want a better life, but countries like Canada, the U.K., Australia (and others) are dealing with the repercussions of an unknown number of radicalized Muslims within their borders. America is no exception.[27] Out of millions who have migrated to Western countries, how many may actually be Islamic militant extremists?

U.S. officials and intelligence agency personnel have publicly acknowledged the existence of radical Islamic sleeper cells in America, which have ties to the Muslim Brotherhood, Hamas and other terrorist groups.[28] Officials have not given the American people specific numbers of how many sleeper cells there are—perhaps to try and mitigate a fearful response. The exact number has been classified. What would we do if these sleeper cells were activated and Islamic militant extremists carried out a coordinated Jihad attack similar to the October 7th attack in Israel or the 2001 September 11th attacks? The 9/11 attacks were committed by 19 militant Islamic extremists who hijacked 4 commercial airliners. These 19 extremists were responsible for the deaths of 2,976 people, with thousands more injured. If 19 men caused such heartache and damage in a coordinated attack, how would we respond to several thousand militant Islamic extremists attacking in America's streets and at key infrastructure locations?

Again, many extremists are vocal about their goals, both in the Middle East and in Western countries: they want "death to America and the conquering of Western civilization." And those extremists who actually live in America, have no problem calling for its destruction. A Qatar-based Muslim cleric, named al Qaradawi, summed up the long-term goals of the radical Islamist ideology at a 1995 conference in Ohio: "...Conquest through Da'wa is what we hope for. We will conquer Europe, we will conquer America! Not through sword, but through Da'wa."[29]

The term Da'wa may be unfamiliar. The term (which can be spelled several ways) is a call for non-Muslims to convert to Islam and for

Muslims to become more devout. However, according to author and human rights activist, Ayaan Hirsi Ali (and based on the context of the above quote from the cleric) the term has a more sinister meaning in the hands of extremist Muslims. "The primary goal of dawa by Islamists is to destroy the political institutions of liberty and replace them with strict Sharia.... In theory, dawa consists of communication and proselytization. In practice, dawa by Islamist groups constitutes a process of radical ideological indoctrination, often under the cover of humanitarian relief work that is connected to jihad."[30]

A growing number within the radical Muslim community have adopted this alternative method to overt violence. This is called "Stealth" or "Civilization" Jihad, and it includes infiltrating a country through immigration to change its landscape. It is a strategy to have the numbers to increasingly influence policies and facilitate the radical Islamic agenda through the use of American media, universities, research centers, activism, political lobbying and deception.[31] This includes attempting to subvert the United States Constitution and local state laws in favor of establishing Islamic Sharia law.[32] A Google search will yield various news and social media results which reveal how this is happening in Michigan, Texas and other states.

Is the stage being set for America to be attacked from both outside and within? We must wake up to this issue so we are not blindsided.

It's one thing for a Muslim to immigrate to this country in search of a better life that is in line with the U.S. Constitution and the American dream. It's another thing entirely if a Muslim comes to this country with the deliberate intention of dismantling America from the inside, in order to recreate it in the image of the Muslim nation which they left. This type of Muslim is a militant extremist—a radical Islamist—the kind we need to protect ourselves against. Given the growing rhetoric from these groups, it stands to reason that plans may be in the works for future attacks. Radical Islam's centuries-long assault on Judaism, Christianity and democracy continues into the future as its proponents seek dominance in every part of the world.

In Revelation 6, which deals with future events (that may be right at our doorstep), 4 horses with 4 riders are released on the earth. What follows is a time of conquering, war, famine and death. This imagery of the horses and riders, that represent tragic events which affect the global population of earth, are known as The Four Horsemen of the Apocalypse. In chapter 53 of his book, **The Dragon's Prophecy:** *Israel, the Dark Resurrection and the End of Days,* Rabbi Jonathan Cahn makes an interesting observation. At the end of the chapter he states:

"So, the Palestinian flag, the flag that was created to nullify the nation of Israel, the flag that is waved around the world in rage against the nation of Israel, just happens to bear the four colors of the four horses of the four horsemen of the apocalypse. Not only that, but the nations of the world that fly these four colors on their flags are almost exclusively the same that have opposed the Jewish nation, that have actively waged war against it, or that are prophesied to do so at the end of the age—white, red, black, and green, the colors of Palestine, the colors of October 7, and—the apocalypse."[33]

Could this observation actually be true? Could there be a connection between The Four Horsemen of the Apocalypse and radical Islam? Revelation 6:9-11 tells us that during the years leading up to Christ's return the result of the horsemen's activities—included in the deaths of millions—will be the martyrdom of God's people: many Christians and Jews.

Pastor Josh Howerton of Lakepointe Church, makes a similar observation based on Revelation 20:4. This verse indicates that many martyrs of the faith will be beheaded. Pastor Josh raises the question in one of his YouTube videos: *Could this Scripture be an indication that radical Islamic extremists will play a major role in End Times events?*[34] Why the question? Historically, the preferred killing method for Muslims has not been suicide bombings, but the beheading of their enemies.

In Joel Richardson's book, The Islamic Antichrist, Richardson quotes several Muslim scholars who state that according to the End Times teachings of Islam, their awaited Mahdi—their messiah figure—is in fact the rider on the white horse in Revelation 6.[35] The problem with this is that according to the Bible, the rider on the white horse is most likely the Antichrist.

These are three different observations from three different Christian leaders. Are they true? Time will tell. But, what we **can** know today is that this militant movement of radical Islam shows no signs of slowing down at all! Rather, it is increasing in intensity in the Middle East and has begun to sweep through Western nations. Islamic militant extremists believe they can and should conquer the entire world in the name of their prophet and Allah. Because of their ideology, rhetoric, overt and covert violence, we should take them seriously and decide how we are going to respond.

Muslims from the Middle East can trace their lineage all the way back to Ishmael, the eldest son of Abraham. In Genesis 16: 11-12, God indicates that Ishmael will live in continual conflict with everyone around him. When we view history past and present, we see the reality of this declaration playing out down through the generations.

While there are definitely other groups to watch out for and stand against—like local gangs, the mob and drug cartels, Neo-Nazis and the Klu Klux Klan, sex-traffickers, Communists, etc—Islamic militant extremists pose a serious threat to every non-Muslim (and peaceful Muslim). These jihadists groups have one stated goal based on how they interpret their religion and its scriptures: that all people everywhere convert to their version of Islam… or pay the tributary tax… or die. It would be wise for us to recognize that there may be extremists living among us and determine how we will respond.[36]

This brings us to the sixth element of The Perfect Storm: APOPHIS.

While we are busy dealing with the daily responsibilities of our own personal lives and the concerns of Deception and the Occult, A.I., Globalism, Transhumanism, and Islamic Extremism; there is a potential existential threat heading towards earth from the stars. Apophis is coming and it doesn't care what our ideological differences may be.

Apophis is the name of an asteroid that is set to allegedly pass by earth on a very close approach on Friday April 13, 2029. If it doesn't hit earth at that time, it may pass by again in 2036—although much farther away. The asteroid was discovered by astronomers at the Kitt Peak National Observatory on June 19, 2004. They named it "Apophis" after the Egyptian serpent god of chaos, darkness and destruction. *(Why would someone use that name?)* Sounds very similar to the biblical description given to Satan in Revelation 12:9. There he is called the great dragon and ancient serpent.

The asteroid has a diameter of 1,115 feet and a length of 1,480 feet. It is almost 5 football fields in length. Its size is comparable to the height of the Empire State Building in NYC or the Eiffel Tower in France!

In December 2004, astronomers became alarmed when the asteroid's trajectory was calculated. At the time, they thought there was a slight possibility that it might hit earth. NASA has since stated that after recalculating, they concluded Apophis would not hit earth, but would rather pass by our planet at 19,600 miles above the surface of the earth. In astronomical terms, this is an extremely small distance! For context, the moon is 238, 900 miles from earth. The geosynchronous satellites we use for broadcast communications, cell phones and GPS circle the planet at around 22,000 miles above the earth. So, Apophis will come closer to the earth's surface than many of our satellites! On that day, it will be visible to the naked eye.

This is important because if NASA's calculations are off, even by a few percentage points, we could be looking at a direct hit to our planet. This is also important because NASA, as well as space agencies from other countries have actively begun working on various types of planetary defense options to stop or alter the course of incoming asteroids. For example, on November 24, 2021 there was a joint project launch between NASA and the Johns Hopkins University Applied Physics Laboratory. It was a space mission named, Double Asteroid Redirection Test (DART). Their goal was to determine how much momentum was needed to deflect or alter an asteroid's trajectory.

They launched the DART spacecraft and targeted a small asteroid, named Dimorphos. On September 26, 2022, the DART spacecraft crashed into the asteroid and did deflect it. Do you remember viewing the story on the news?[37] Is this just a coincidence? Are space agencies merely preparing for a *future possibility that might come one day?* Or, could the reality be they are making preparations to try and deflect Apophis because it ***is*** on a collision course for earth?

Could this also be the reason why there is such a push to get back to the moon by 2027 and out to Mars between 2029-2031?[38] Are scientists looking at options for moving off-world in case of a major asteroid collision? And what about the huge spike in underground bunker building for the wealthy? While bunkers would help protect people from warfare scenarios, is Apophis also a consideration?

Since we are not privy to private government and NASA meetings, we don't know anything beyond public record. But, if you've watched movies like Armageddon, Deep Impact, Don't Look Up, Greenland, the tv show Salvation, and others, then you know telling the world population too soon, that an asteroid will hit the planet, would cause anarchy, chaos and pandemonium. No. It's better not to say something until a viable plan can be put in place to help ensure the survival of the human race, animal and plant lifeforms on earth. Only those who absolutely need to know, would be informed.

Then there's the creation of the 6th branch of the U.S. military: the Space Force. Many people scoffed and laughed at the announcement in 2019, but could key government personnel know something about Apophis that they are not saying? The Space Force will work to protect America's interests in space with satellite weaponry. Apophis being on a possible collision course with earth would serve as great motivation to get these protective systems operational!

Is this what's happening now? Stop and think for a moment. At the writing of this book, April 13, 2029 is 3.5 years away. That's a little more than 1,200 days from now. In his January 24, 2013 article, then CNN Science writer, Greg Bear stated the following about Apophis:

"...Scientists have revised their worst estimates of its chances of striking Earth. Current thinking is: We're safe... There's always the possibility we don't have these measurements exactly right. Something could happen at any point in Apophis' orbit to modify its course, just a smidgen... Apophis masses at more than 20 million tons. If it hit Earth, the impact would unleash a blast the equivalent of over a billion tons of TNT. That's not an extinction event, but it could easily cause billions of deaths and months, if not years, of climate disruption. The potential risk is huge."[39]

This is also significant because the Bible, in Revelation chapter 8:7-12, tells us of a future time when an asteroid/comet will hit the earth and cause cataclysmic damage. For the sake of space, we'll only look at verses 7-9:

7 *The first angel sounded his trumpet, and there came hail and fire mixed with blood, and it was hurled down on the earth. A third of the earth was burned up, a third of the trees were burned up, and all the green grass was burned up.* **8** *The second angel sounded his trumpet, and something like a huge mountain, all ablaze, was thrown into the sea. A third of the sea turned into blood,* **9** *a third of the living creatures in the sea died, and a third of the ships were destroyed."*

This reads like the beginning of a multi-stage impact, where pieces of an asteroid/comet break off ahead of the main body and hit the earth first—with the main body following closely behind. The question is, **could the asteroid Apophis, which is currently on its way to earth, be on a collision course with our planet?** Could it be *the* "something like a huge mountain, all ablaze" that the apostle John sees in a vision of the future? If it is, Revelation states this will be a cataclysmic event which will serve as one aspect of God's judgment against the inhabitants of the earth who have consistently rebelled against Him.

Apophis hitting the earth in 2029 could be a very real possibility. Even if its current trajectory sets it to "just miss" us, what if something—like the gravitational pull of a nearby planet or an impact of some kind—causes it to shift trajectory between now and 2029? A shift that puts it on a collision course with earth? What should we do to prepare for this possibility? Should we be concerned enough—at least—to learn as much as we can about Apophis *before* April 13, 2029? Or should we dismiss the possibility altogether and just focus on "ground level" duties and problems of our day-to-day living?

CONCLUSION

In meteorology the term, "perfect storm" refers to a powerful storm created by a convergence of several rare and unusual atmospheric conditions. Figuratively speaking, a "perfect storm" refers to a situation where multiple adverse elements or events combine to create a much worse circumstance than any single factor could have done alone. This chapter has highlighted 6 factors of global consequence. Each factor is rare, unusual and potentially adverse by itself. Yet, they are all happening and converging together in the world within the same timeframe. These 6 factors are not the only ones. Rather, they are the ones I have chosen to raise in this book. We can also include other factors such as the global increase of warfare, natural disasters and lawlessness. According to the Bible, all of these will converge together as the return of Christ draws near. Some will say there have always been wars and natural disasters. This is why I have focused on these 6 other factors, because we should all be able to agree that their presence has increased in notable ways in recent years. Even secular pundits note these unusual trends and are unsure what to make of them. Yet, while people grow increasingly fearful, the Scriptures reveal the reality behind the things we are all experiencing.
So, what's the bottom line? Again, while we are busy living our lives, Deception and the Occult, Artificial Intelligence, Globalism, Transhumanism, Militant Islamic Extremism, and the Apophis asteroid are swirling all around us. They are converging into the perfect storm. This will be a storm that will affect entire regions and the world itself. All of these can be traced back to biblical prophecy. Again, Dr. Sampson states in his book, Revelation Now, *"Conflicts in the book of Revelation are not regional but global."*[40]

We are living in the days of Revelation. Where exactly are we? I believe somewhere between chapter 3 and the opening of the seals in Revelation 6.

Jesus has revealed to us what will happen so we can get right with God while we still have time. Some of us may die before all of these factors fully converge. Some of us may be alive to experience the full ramifications of this perfect storm. Either way, we should look at what's happening in the world (beyond our day-to-day-bubble) and seriously consider what is coming and what is already here. This will help us live life on purpose… to *respond* and not merely react. Although it may look like the world is spinning out of control—and in many ways it is—what we must remember is this: if God has told us ahead of time what will happen, then He must also be in control!

So, as you consider these words, my prayer is that you will place your faith in Jesus Christ as your Lord, King and Savior. May you seek to have a solid, vibrant relationship with Him by studying His Word (the Bible), obeying His teachings, and preparing for His return. Death comes to us all. If we have a relationship with Jesus, then He promises at the moment of our death, He will be waiting to welcome us into His eternal Kingdom.

While these 6 signs may be frightening, later in this book, we will look at a 7th sign, which should provide you with some hope. So, keep reading! But before we get there, we must take a look at a future time which will rock the inhabitants of the earth.

CHAPTER 2

THE COMING TRIBULATION

When the Bible speaks of Jesus' Second Coming, it references a critical timeframe in human history that we call, The Tribulation. This period spans 7 years and culminates with Jesus' return to earth as the rightful Creator, Savior, King, Lord and Judge of the world. In essence, these 7 years are the last humanity will have before God brings His heavenly Kingdom here to earth in all of its fullness.

The Tribulation, also mentioned in Jeremiah 30:7 as "the time of Jacob's trouble," *centers* around Israel and other countries in the Middle East. However, according to the book of Revelation and other scriptural passages, the ramifications of the Tribulation will impact the entire world. Speaking of this time in Matthew 24, Jesus refers to the prophet Daniel by name: revealing that the prophecies and experiences written by Daniel are necessary for us to understand how the Tribulation unfolds. (See Daniel chapters 2, 3, 7-12)

We must take a moment to review a foundational passage: Daniel 9:24-27. It is here that God sends the high-ranking angel, Gabriel to Daniel to reveal a key prophecy about the Messiah's coming and the future of Israel and the world. Since, entire books have been written on these verses, I will only give a basic 3-point summary of what they mean. Here is the prophecy:

—

24 *"Seventy 'sevens' (weeks of years) are decreed for your people and your holy city to finish transgression, to put an end to sin, to atone for wickedness, to bring in everlasting righteousness, to seal up vision and prophecy and to anoint the Most Holy Place.*

25 *"Know and understand this: From the time the word goes out to restore and rebuild Jerusalem until the Anointed One, the ruler, comes, there will be* *seven 'sevens,' and sixty-two 'sevens.' It will be rebuilt with streets and a trench, but in times of trouble.* **26** *After the sixty-two 'sevens,' the Anointed One will be put to death and will have nothing. The people of the ruler who will come will destroy the city and the sanctuary. The end will come like a flood: War will continue until the end, and desolations have been decreed.*

27 *He will confirm a covenant with many for one 'seven.' In the middle of the 'seven' he will put an end to sacrifice and offering. And at the temple he will set up an abomination that causes desolation, until the end that is decreed is poured out on him."*

—

First: The language of "sevens/weeks/years" may seem confusing to the uninitiated. The 70 weeks equal 490 years. Gabriel says this total timeframe has been set to accomplish six goals: to finish transgression, to put an end to sin, to atone for wickedness, to bring in everlasting righteousness, to seal up vision and prophecy and to anoint the Most Holy Place. Out of these six goals, only one has been fully completed: Jesus' atonement for wickedness. The other five are either partially fulfilled or have yet to be fulfilled. Thus, we see the need for Jesus' Second Coming. As Jesus said in Luke 24:44, *"...Everything must be fulfilled that is written about me in the Law of Moses,* ***the Prophets*** *and the Psalms." (Emphasis mine)*

Second: Gabriel reveals the Messiah will come and be executed— 483 years *(69 weeks)* after the decree for the Jews to leave their captivity and return to their homeland Israel to rebuild Jerusalem. The Bible states this decree was given by the King of Persia, Artaxerxes I. Centuries later—fitting this timeframe exactly—Jesus made His triumphal entry into Jerusalem *(Lk 19:28-44)* and was crucified.

Third: One week remains... But Gabriel mentions an "interlude period" that begins with the destruction of *the city and sanctuary*—stretching into the future for an unrevealed amount of time. *(Jesus also predicted this in Matthew 24).* This interlude began in 70 AD when Rome destroyed Jerusalem, the temple and scattered the Jews to the four corners of the world. It has continued from that time until now *(over 1900 years).* World history confirms these years have been filled with many escalating wars (as Gabriel said it would be).

This timeframe is also called the Church age—where God's grace has been extended to the gentile nations of the world so everyone can have an opportunity to hear the gospel and receive Christ as Lord and Savior. According to Jesus *(Matthew 24:14)* and the Apostle Paul *(Romans 11:25)*, this grace period has an expiration date. Once reached, the interlude will end. **Then**, the last week of the prophecy will commence. The 7 years of the Tribulation will be upon us.

Again, this is just an overview. If you want to dive deeper, I recommend the book, *Daniel's 70 Weeks*, by the late Dr. Chuck Missler.

Now, let's take a closer look at the Tribulation...

The Bible reveals The Tribulation is divided into three distinct sections. During the first 3.5 years, the Antichrist will arrive on the world stage as a kind of mysterious charismatic political savior. He will seem to have all the answers to society's ills. He will bring "peace and safety" to regions—such as the Middle East—where it has been elusive for generations. This will include brokering or strengthening an agreement that's already in place between the Jews and Muslims. This agreement will allow the Jews to rebuild their Jewish temple and resume animal sacrifices according to Old Testament law. During this time the Antichrist will also accumulate unparalleled political and military power. The majority of the world population will come to idolize him. He will be encouraged to take control of the planet's governing systems and he will gladly accept this invitation.[1]

Jesus, the prophet Daniel and the apostle Paul reveal that 3.5 years into the Tribulation, a *distinct event* will take place. It is called, ***"the Abomination which causes desolation"*** and it will reveal the Antichrist's true intentions to the world. At this point he will walk into the Jewish temple in Jerusalem and do three things: 1) He will cause the animal sacrificial system to cease. 2) He will enter the most holy place of the temple, declare himself to be God and demand to be worshipped by all. 3) He will call for an all-out-war against Jews, Christians and anyone else who refuses to pledge allegiance to him, his government and his worship system.[2]

The global chaos that follows is, what Jesus refers to as, the worst time of persecution and suffering in all of human history![3] This period is known as the **"Great Tribulation."** Think about that for a moment… Jesus' warning means all previous wars, genocides and calamities will pale in comparison to what is coming, once the Antichrist assumes control of the earth. Every evil dictator—from Mao Zedong, to Joseph Stalin, to Adolf Hitler and others—who were responsible for the murder of over 160 million people, will be like schoolyard bullies compared to the unimaginable atrocities the Antichrist will unleash. This is a sobering reality to consider… So, the first division in the 7 year Tribulation—the abomination which causes desolation—happens right down the middle at the 3.5 year mark.

A third division will happen *within the second half* of the Tribulation. At some point during the Great Tribulation a series of major events will unfold. The Bible calls this, **"The Day of the LORD."** This is when God pours out His wrath on a world population that has refused Him and pledged its allegiance to the Antichrist. These judgments will decimate the global antichrist system and those who follow, support and seek to protect it. God's judgments will also prepare the way for Jesus' world-wide return to earth and the war of Armageddon. It is here in the plains of Megiddo *(the Jezreel Valley in northern Israel)* where the Antichrist will gather earth's armies together in a futile attempt to fight against Christ. They will lose![4]

So, this 7 year period referred to as, The Tribulation, is actually made up of 3 distinct parts: The time of "Peace and Safety." The Great Tribulation. The Day of the LORD.

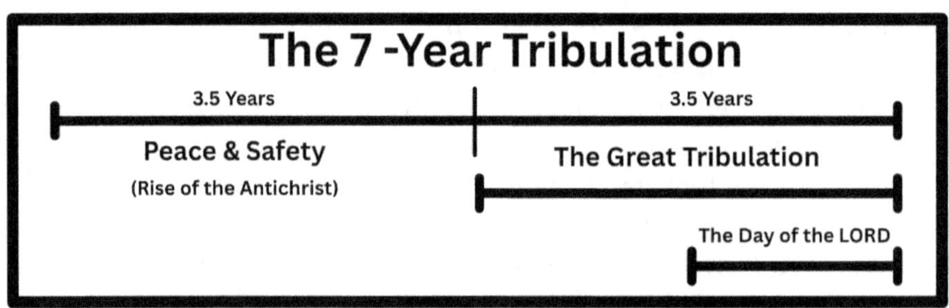

THE DECENT DOWNWARD

Scripture reveals that God will allow the devil to deceive a world that has repeatedly rebelled against truth. God will give an unbelieving humanity over to a great delusion of their own making: they can be their own gods. And God will allow them to receive the greatest liar of all: Satan himself, who will claim to be god.[5]

We can already see society heading down this slippery slope. The love of evil, occult practices and ungodly behavior is rising exponentially as lawlessness increases worldwide. This will ultimately prepare the way for the "man of lawlessness." Time and time again, what used to be said in private is boldly declared in public: *"we don't need God. We can be our own gods! We will create a god after our own image!"*

According to the Bible, human history is not headed toward a man-made utopia in the heavens, rather it is descending to a demonically devised dystopia. The book of Revelation does not indicate that John was given a vision of *one possible future* where the Antichrist rules—and thus we can change that outcome by making different choices. No. Revelation indicates the future John saw is in fact **our** future that is to come. *That future* is the sum total of all of the decisions humanity has and continues to make. The Tribulation is almost upon us!

A PRECURSOR TO THE TRIBULATION

The Bible reveals a major precursor to the start of the Tribulation… something to indicate that we are almost at its door: the great apostasy. In 2 Thessalonians 2:3, the apostle Paul lets us know that many in the Church will turn away from faith in Jesus…

The Apostasy: for the last several decades the world has witnessed an increasing exodus from the Christian faith. Countless people who once walked with Christ and proclaimed His Word, have turned away from Christ and gone back to living lives devoid of Him. From regular everyday people to church leaders and pastors, to notable personalities, people across the world have and are turning away from the faith. While there are many other precursors (some of which

I have mentioned), this apostasy is the most telling about where we are in human history as it relates to the start of the 7 year Tribulation. We are close indeed.

WHEN DOES THIS BEGIN?

This truth is undeniable. The signs are all around us. The Tribulation is coming. We are almost at its door. Now, the question is: how can we tell when the Tribulation has actually begun?

A major debate has been taking place for centuries within Christendom. It centers on The Rapture: *the biblical teaching that at some point Jesus will return suddenly to remove His Church from the earth.* The primary focus of the debate is on the *timing:* when does it happen? There are 3 widely known views.

Some believe in a "Pre-Tribulation" timing: that Jesus raptures the Church before the Tribulation, which then kicks off all of the unfolding drama. Other Christians believe in a "Mid-Tribulation" timing: that Jesus raptures the Church at the midway point just before the Great Tribulation begins (when things get *really* bad). Still, others believe in a "Post-Tribulation" timing: that Jesus raptures the Church at the very end of the Tribulation. There is also a lesser-known 4th view. It is called the "Pre-Wrath" timing: that Jesus raptures the church at some point during the second half of the 7 years, just before God's wrath is poured out on an unbelieving world.

Unfortunately, there is no major consensus on which view is correct. So, I would encourage you to do your own research. *(If you want to understand my belief on this subject, you can read my article in the Appendix.)* So, since the timing issue can be a point of contention, I will use other indicators which can let us know when the Tribulation has begun.

ONE: A treaty of peace between Israel and the Muslim nations which surround it is established.

TWO: The priesthood in Jerusalem re-establishes the animal sacrificial system described in the Old Testament.

THREE: A third Jewish temple is built in Jerusalem, on or near the Dome of the Rock.

FOUR: The two witnesses of Revelation 11 show up in Israel and begin to proclaim the gospel and perform signs and wonders.

Any two of these four things taking place would signal the 7 year Tribulation has begun. Right now, there are major efforts underway (through the United Nations, Abraham Accords, Jared Kushner, etc) to try and ensure peace and security in the Middle East. Meanwhile, there is a group in Jerusalem, called the Temple Institute, which is prepared to begin animal sacrifices and build a third Jewish temple. They only lack: a red heifer that meets Torah requirements (which must be sacrificed first), rabbinical and governmental clearances and the actual land to do so.[6]

So, three out of four of the signs I've listed are actively being pursued right now. Is that a coincidence? Or are we closer than we think to the start of the Tribulation? These are questions to seriously consider.

THE TECHNOLOGY OF THE TRIBULATION

In addition to these things, the Bible gives a clear snapshot of what society will look like during the time of the tribulation. This is found in Revelation chapters 11 and 13, which hold special significance because they provide technological indicators. The book of Revelation was written by the apostle John around 95 AD. The chapters I am referencing are visions of the future God gave John. What John described bears a striking resemblance to our modern day technological age.

It's important that we pause here...

Over the years, I have heard several Bible teachers downplay this connection. They have strongly suggested technological development is not at all a factor in the book of Revelation. They have also claimed the Mark of the Beast in Revelation 13 is not a technological mark, but rather it is solely an invisible spiritual marking.

This type of teaching is dangerous because it fosters a disconnect. It leads believers to think if a technological mark is forced on society, they can go ahead and receive it, because ***the Mark*** is only spiritual. But, Revelation is clear: those who take the mark are forever lost and cannot be redeemed.[7] So, it is important for us to examine this aspect because the similarities between the technology being created and what we see in Revelation 13 are simply too close to be coincidence.

Dr. John Lennox, speaks all over the world on biblical and scientific truth. In a video interview about his latest book on God, A.I. and Revelation, he shared a quote from his friend and mentor Robert Edward David Clark. Mr. Clark was a British chemist and devout Christian who took the Bible and science seriously. In reference to the book of Revelation, Dr. Lennox quotes Mr. Clark as saying:

"If we really believe that Revelation is, in part at least as it says a prophecy, and it does talk about the future... Why should we always try to interpret it using imagery or things in the real world from the past? God must have foreseen the technological age [which was to come]."[8]

I agree with this statement. The book of Revelation ends with Jesus' return and the creation of a new universe. Since those things have not happened yet, that means we are STILL in Bible days! So, when John wrote down the visions of Revelation, the future he saw had to include our own. Therefore, it is my belief that the Mark of the Beast will be technological AND spiritual in nature. I will unpack this a bit more. **So, let's unpause and continue...**

In speaking of the time during the Tribulation, the apostle John references global communication, global tracking, global commerce and global worship. For an example, let's look at Revelation 11:7-10.

7 *"Now when they [the two witnesses] have finished their testimony, the beast that comes up from the Abyss will attack them, and overpower and kill* *them.* ***8*** *Their bodies will lie in the public square of the great city—which is figuratively called Sodom and Egypt—where also their Lord was crucified.* ***9*** *For three and a half days some from every people, tribe, language and nation will gaze on their bodies and refuse them burial.* ***10*** *The inhabitants of the earth will gloat over them and will celebrate by sending each other gifts, because these two prophets had tormented those who live on the earth."*

Notice the whole world celebrates the killing of God's two witnesses in Jerusalem. The only way this is possible is through global digital technology. Onlookers in Jerusalem will watch as the Antichrist overpowers God's witnesses. The entire exchange will be captured on video and shared with the world. This would not have been possible in previous generations. The technology simply had not been created yet. But we now live in the age of social media where instantaneous live video feeds can be beamed around the world in minutes.

In her book, *The Age of Surveillance Capitalism: The Fight for a Human Future at the New Frontier of Power*, Dr. Shoshana Zuboff tracks the rise of social media and the global surveillance state. She quotes Alex Pentland, a prolific author, data science researcher, and advisor to top business CEOs and global heads of government. Dr. Zuboff shares a 2011 essay written by Petland, where he says:

"We must create a nervous system for humanity that maintains the stability of our societies' systems throughout the globe… For the first time in history, the majority of humanity is linked… As a consequence, our mobile wireless infrastructure can be 'reality mined' in order to… monitor our environments, and plan the development of our society… Reality mining of the 'digital breadcrumbs' left behind as we go about our daily lives offers the potential for creating remarkable, second-by-second models of group dynamics and reactions over extended periods of time… In short, we now have the capacity to collect and analyze data about people with a breadth and depth that was previously inconceivable."[9]

This line of thinking sounds similar to Dr. Ben Goertzle's quote from chapter 1. I share this to demonstrate that the technological infrastructure needed to mirror what we read in Revelation 11 is already here! And the technology needed to mirror Revelation 13 is currently being created as we speak.

All of this is tied together by an identification mark on the right hand and/or forehead of each person who wishes to participate in this global system overseen by the Antichrist. What John describes almost 2000 years ago, bears striking resemblance to the world we have and are currently creating through the Internet and a wide array of digital technologies. Again, can this be merely a coincidence?

There are wireless RFID chip implants that up to 100,000 people worldwide have already inserted in their bodies. The implant is the size of a grain of rice and carries financial and medical information. No need for wallets and credit cards anymore. It can also lock/unlock smart-enabled devices.[10]

Then there's Elon Musk's Neural Link brain-computer interface (BCI) device that will be inserted underneath the skull. It's the size of a coin and is supposed to help people who are paralyzed to control external smart devices with their thoughts. It will also be used to treat neurological disorders and enhance human capabilities. The device is now in the early stages of human trials.[11]

But what will happen when Neural Link becomes available to the public? What will happen when people can connect their brains directly to the Internet? Can you imagine no longer needing a phone to surf the web, buy and sell, and to control smart devices? What will it be like to do all of that, and more, at the speed of thought? And what happens when you can connect yourself directly to the pinnacle of our technological innovation: artificial intelligence? We already looked at some of the dangers in chapter 1—and that's without being directly connected to the Internet!

Digital communication is a two-way street. What's to stop those who control the technology from extracting information from the minds connected to these systems? Or worse, actually controlling their personalities and actions? At the point when people merge with the Machine, what will it mean to be human? Will they still be human?

These two technologies I have mentioned above may not be the exact iterations of The Mark of the Beast in Revelation 13, but they sure bear a striking resemblance to it. Can that merely be a coincidence? Is there biblically, "nothing to see here?" Is this not connected at all to what the apostle John said was coming in our future? We may not want to admit that the connection exists… but with all of this similarity how could we not? Have the "tech giants" built—and are continuing to build the technology that will be used to enslave us during the time of the Tribulation? Have we—in fact—crossed the "technological tipping point?" I don't want to say it… but I'm afraid so. We are moving at breakneck speed towards a world where everything, everyplace and everyone is digitally tracked, monitored and regulated. There is no going back. There is only moving forward.

Let's pause here for a moment… I know this may be a lot to take in. Take a minute to breathe. Stand up. Stretch. Go get something to drink. Say a prayer. Then come back so I can share a somewhat comical story with you.

When I was a teenager, my friends and I went to a haunted house attraction at a carnival. The haunted house was a long trailer where you entered on one side and exited on the other. It had all of the necessary trappings: the smoke, strobe lights, scary organ music and ghoulish imagery painted on the walls. While we waited our turn, we could hear the screaming and sinister cackling inside. I didn't want to go in, but my friends pressured me. They said, if we stay together as a group, we'll be okay!

Once we got inside—in the pitch black—my friends left me! They ran to the exit as fast as they could! I was terrified, turned around and tried to go back out through the door we had entered, but it was locked from the outside! So… I had to go forward… I cried and screamed my way through that entire experience as people dressed as ghosts, demons and axe murderers did their best to scare me half-to-death! I was so happy when I finally emerged through the exit and saw daylight! Here I am now, in my early 50s, and I can remember that experience as if it happened yesterday!

Why am I sharing this with you? Because in that situation, I had to face my fears. You and I will have to do the same with the issue of the coming Tribulation. We can't go back. We have to go forward. And we must trust that if we move forward with Jesus as our Savior, Lord, Guide, Comforter, Protector and Sustainer, we will make it through whatever darkness we encounter and get to the daylight on the other side! So, while hearing about all of this technology may cause some anxiety, remember that God told us about this ahead of time, so we can be prepared to stand firm until the end. Because, as Jesus says in Matthew 24:13, those who endure to the end will be saved! So, don't give up! Keep pressing forward! **Let's unpause and continue...**

Interestingly, in Revelation 13, John describes an "image" being created in the likeness of the Antichrist. This image is given "breath" so that it is animated and can speak, think and act. This "image" is able to monitor the entire global system in real time in order to keep track of every citizen that is plugged into the system—as well as help to limit access and hunt down those who refuse to participate in the global system. Let's take a look at the entire chapter:

—

1 *The dragon stood on the shore of the sea. And I saw a beast coming out of*
the sea. It had ten horns and seven heads, with ten crowns on its horns, and
on each head a blasphemous name. **2** *The beast I saw resembled a leopard, but*
had feet like those of a bear and a mouth like that of a lion. The dragon gave
the beast his power and his throne and great authority. **3** *One of the heads of*
the beast seemed to have had a fatal wound, but the fatal wound had been
healed. The whole world was filled with wonder and followed the beast.
4 *People worshiped the dragon because he had given authority to the beast,*
and they also worshiped the beast and asked, "Who is like the beast? Who can
wage war against it?"

5 *The beast was given a mouth to utter proud words and blasphemies and to*
exercise its authority for forty-two months. **6** *It opened its mouth to*
blaspheme God, and to slander his name and his dwelling place and those
who live in heaven. **7** *It was given power to wage war against God's holy*
people and to conquer them. And it was given authority over every tribe,
people, language and nation. **8** *All inhabitants of the earth will worship the*

beast—all whose names have not been written in the Lamb's book of life, the
Lamb who was slain from the creation of the world.

9 *Whoever has ears, let them hear.* **10** *"If anyone is to go into captivity, into*
captivity they will go. If anyone is to be killed with the sword, with the sword
they will be killed." This calls for patient endurance and faithfulness on the
part of God's people.

The Beast out of the Earth

11 *Then I saw a second beast, coming out of the earth. It had two horns like a*
lamb, but it spoke like a dragon. **12** *It exercised all the authority of the first*
beast on its behalf, and made the earth and its inhabitants worship the first
beast, whose fatal wound had been healed. **13** *And it performed great signs,*
even causing fire to come down from heaven to the earth in full view of the
people.

14 *Because of the signs it was given power to perform on behalf of the first*
beast, it deceived the inhabitants of the earth. It ordered them to set up an
image in honor of the beast who was wounded by the sword and yet lived.
15 *The second beast was given power to give breath to the image of the first*
beast, so that the image could speak and cause all who refused to worship the
image to be killed. **16** *It also forced all people, great and small, rich and poor,*
free and slave, to receive a mark on their right hands or on their foreheads,
17 *so that they could not buy or sell unless they had the mark, which is the*
name of the beast or the number of its name.

18 *This calls for wisdom. Let the person who has insight calculate the*
number of the beast, for it is the number of a man. That number is 666.
—

There's a lot that can be said about this chapter. However, that would exceed the scope of this book. But let me highlight a few things. 1) The dragon is Satan. 2) The beast from the sea is both the Antichrist and the kingdom he rules. 3) The beast from the earth (land) is the false prophet. 4) The image is some kind of robotic statue. I know, saying a "robotic statue" sounds crazy. But let me explain.

In 2008, while reading this chapter, I prayed: "LORD, what is the "breath" that is given to the image?" God's response was immediate and clear as day: "Artificial Intelligence." Up until that time, in my mind, Artificial intelligence was relegated to science fiction movies like The Terminator and The Matrix. I never thought about it within the context of biblical eschatology.

In my mind, I saw the "breath" in purely spiritual terms. I imagined a statue, like the one King Nebuchadnezzar built in Daniel 3, where he demanded the citizens of his kingdom to worship it. I imagined something like that harboring a demonic entity within it. But, here was God revealing that technology had a major role to play in this great deception. It blew my mind! Could this be true?

At that time, outside of science fiction circles, very few were publicly talking about Artificial Intelligence. Now, in 2025, it's practically all we talk about! Artificial intelligence is upon us, growing at rates faster than its creators can keep up with. It is touted as humanity's last greatest invention that will change everything and enable possibilities we can't even imagine yet.

Is what I heard from God, correct? Will the "breath" given to the Image of the Beast be Artificial Intelligence? Interestingly, other Christian thinkers, apologists and scholars have arrived at similar conclusions. If this is true, then the "image of the beast," which is foreshadowed in Daniel 3, will be some type of robotic-android-avatar that is powered by A.I. and fully integrated into the Internet—and everything connected to it. This Image will be a kind of digital doppelgänger of the Antichrist that will enable him to have near omnipresence in a global dictatorship. And similar to The Terminator, The Matrix, I Robot and Avengers: Age of Ultron, a central "robotic image" can be linked to hundreds and even thousands of copies of itself—all operating as One.

I know… this sounds unbelievable! But is it? Cell phones (and video conferencing on them) seemed farfetched 30 years ago. Now, we take them for granted! A "robotic image" may seem implausible now, but just look at the cutting-edge robotic technology currently being developed by companies like, Hanson Robotics, Boston Dynamics, Tesla, 1X and even Disney (just to name a few). Thanks to billions of dollars in investments, the technology continues to improve at accelerated rates. Thanks to AI, robots can walk, run, crawl, dance, jump, flip, punch, kick, etc. Also, according to a 60 Minutes special on humanoid robots *(Jan 2026)*, when a robot learns a new skill, that learning can be uploaded to all the other robots connected the same network. This enables them to perform the skill as well, without having to "learn it." So, it's not far-fetched to see how a "robotic image" that operates like the description in Revelation 13 could become reality.

The signs are all around us. This is what we are creating. One more thing. Chapter 13 tells us that without the Mark, people can't "buy or sell." Think about it. For the system which exists in this chapter to work, it must be cashless—digital. That is the only way every person on the planet can be monitored in real time and "locked out" if they don't have the mark.

This sounds like the system that's presently being created all around us. Think Amazon's hand pay system at Whole Foods as a precursor to what's coming. It's called Amazon One, which is a biometric payment method where customers link their palm print to a credit card and Amazon account for quick, wallet-free checkout. All you do is hover your palm over the scanner device to pay for your groceries. (This is just one example!)

The difference is that—in Revelation 13—the digital system is complete and fully operational. One day, during the Covid Pandemic, my father and I were discussing Revelation 13. He made an observation: *"When the Internet is complete, the Antichrist will come."* I was stunned. It was like the thought just hit him, he uttered it and the conversation continued without any elaboration.

If you research the "Internet of Things," you will discover that the vision for the Internet (of the future) has not yet been fully realized. In order to have the level of digitization that can handle a robust global virtual system of augmented and virtual reality (and more), new components are being added to the Internet infrastructure every day to increase power, connectivity and range.

A more powerful "net" is coming… We have always created technology to amplify our physical and mental abilities. We are now creating technological systems that will amplify the capabilities of those who oversee them—and ultimately—of "the one" who will oversee it all.

When I think about how humanity is uniting through the "language" of science and technology, I am reminded of the Tower of Babel incident in Genesis 11. There, our ancestors—unified by one language—sought to create their version of utopia by building a tower to the heavens. This was in complete defiance of God's will. God eventually came down and stopped them. Here we are in our day… Things have almost come full circle. We're gathering together in defiance of God once again. God will most surely come down. At Christ's second coming He will settle things once-and-for-all!

WHERE DO WE GO FROM HERE?

It is not possible to turn the clock back. We are time travelers who can only go forward one second at a time. The visions given to John the apostle were not *"one possible future"* that we can somehow avoid by making different choices. It is the future that's coming. And everything we do to change it actually makes it come even quicker. It is inevitable.

So, if the Tribulation is inevitable, then where do we go from here? What do we do? Every generation faced a crucible. And God's proclamation has always been the same: place your faith and trust in Him! He is your ultimate Source for purpose, meaning and significance. This proclamation does not change in our modern day. Here are 5 things we should do in light of the future that's approaching:

—The first and most important thing for us to do is place our faith in Jesus and trust Him for the outcome of our lives.

—The second thing for us to do is to live out loud: share the gospel with others through your words and actions. Be witnesses unto Jesus wherever He plants you in life. Let those who do not believe in Christ see Christ in you. And help your fellow sisters and brothers in Christ to grow in their relationship with Him.

—The third thing for us to do is to keep track of and enjoy God's blessings every day. God never stops blessing His children. And He is not restricted to only providing blessings in good times.[12] In fact, many of His greatest blessings to us come in times of persecution and great difficulty. How else would we know God is a great Deliverer and Sustainer if we had nothing to be delivered from and sustained through?

—The fourth thing you can do is physically and mentally prepare for what's coming. In what ways can you become self-sufficient? Do you have any food, drink and medical resources saved up in case of emergency? Do you know how to live off the land if you need to? If not, do you know others who do? Could you team up if necessary?

Have you thought through what technological lines you won't cross? If not, then when the Mark of the Beast arrives and everyone is told to take it if they want to be able to buy groceries, have healthcare, get jobs, etc, then you may cave under the heavy weight of global governmental pressure! Determine how much digital technology is too much technology. Don't be so connected to the system that you can't unplug if it comes down to it. Maintain some mental and spiritual disciplines that do not require any technology at all.

And how is your health? Are you in shape? How much weight can you lift? How far can you walk? If your body is falling apart, you won't survive long living disconnected from the Antichrist governmental system.

A part of mental and spiritual strength is having strong relationships. What kind of network do you have of like-minded believers who are serious about their relationship with Christ and who also want to prepare for the future? What skills do you have? What skills do others in your network have? How can you leverage them if you find yourself in the Tribulation?

—The fifth thing you can do is: LOOK UP! Jesus says in Luke 21 that when we see all of these things happening all around us, look up, because our redemption is drawing near! In other words, all of these difficulties are signs that Jesus is on the way! He will soon return to save us and set everything right in the world. He will soon come to take us home to His heavenly kingdom. And He will soon bring His kingdom right down to the earth. As followers of Christ, Jesus calls us to look up! We are to desire and long for His appearing! We are to realize we are just pilgrims passing through this world... we are *in* this world... but we are no longer *of* this world.

CONCLUSION

The Tribulation is coming. But God tells us to have joy because our ultimate hope is not in this world, but is found in HIM. Some of you may say, "Jesus is going to rapture us out of here before any of these things happen." Believe me, I am all for a "Pre-Tribulation Rapture." I am ready to go home to be with the LORD whenever He is ready for me to come. However, as it was stated earlier, there is no consensus within the Christian community on the timing of the rapture. People have made cases for each possibility: Pre, Mid, Post.

However, I came to the conclusion several years ago that many people's faith in Jesus is tied directly to their belief that He will rapture the Church BEFORE the Tribulation begins. But, what happens if the rapture comes later? What happens if Christians have to go through part or all of the Tribulation? If our faith is tied to Jesus AND the "Pre-Tribulation" rapture, then we will fall apart if the rapture doesn't happen first. *BUT*, if our faith is tied to Jesus alone, then it doesn't matter when the rapture happens. We will be able to endure because our focus is squarely on Christ and His sovereignty over all situations and circumstances—including the Tribulation.

So, keep your eyes on Jesus! Pay attention to the signs listed in this book. Make the preparations that you can do. Trust God to sustain you. If you do these things, you and your family will make a great impact for God's kingdom during this most critical time in all of human history. *(If you are interested in understanding my view of the rapture, please see the article in the appendix.)*

In his book, *Against the Machine: On the Unmaking of Humanity,* Paul Kingsnorth takes the reader on a whirlwind journey through history in order to expose the creation of the Machine that is increasingly enslaving humanity. At the end of the book, when it feels like all hope may be lost, he writes these words:

"I have come to the end now, and here is what I think: that the age of the Machine is not after all a hopeless time. Actually, it is the time we were born for. We can't leave it, so we have to fully inhabit it. We have to understand it, challenge it, resist it, subvert it, walk through it on towards something better. If we can see what it is, we have a duty to speak the words to those who do not yet see, all the while struggling to remain human."[13]

If you are reading these words, then God has you here in today's generation for such a time as this. Although life is growing increasingly dark, it is always darkest before the dawn. No matter how bad things get, it is all a sign that points to the Truth: OUR KING IS COMING! Jesus told us ahead of time so we can be ready. So, let us prepare ourselves and have hope!

CHAPTER 3

THE GREATEST OPPORTUNITY

The title of this book is, The Perfect Storm. This name is used primarily as a meteorological term, which refers to an unusually severe storm that is a result of a rare combination of weather phenomena. In this book, we've been looking at a rare combination of signs Jesus said would converge as the end of the age draws near. Granted, some of these signs weren't mentioned by name in the Bible —like artificial intelligence—but the biblical indicators are present which point to their existence. While these signs may fill us with anxiety, just as a major storm would, we must remember that for all of their destructive power, storms actually do benefit the planet in ways we often don't consider.

Storms: 1) help maintain the global heat balance, 2) provide essential rainfall, 3) clear pollutants from the air and water, 4) promote ecological renewal. In a similar way, the perfect storm of signs that Jesus tells us will happen, while being destructive, do serve a purpose. **The signs:** 1) confront us with the reality of our own mortality, 2) cause us to consider the existence of God, 3) helps us see what truly matters in life and 4) provides us with the opportunity to seriously consider giving our lives to Jesus for eternal salvation.

Without storms, our lives continue on *auto-pilot*. We go about our daily routines, often without giving God any serious thought. We live for ourselves, our dreams, our desires, our agendas. But storms serve as a reminder that ultimately, we are not in control (although we like to think we are the captains of our own fate).

The truth is, storms often wake us up from our stupor. Storms open our eyes to truth we previously did not see, although it was right in front of us the whole time. So, again, while they may bring destruction and loss of life, weather-related storms also serve to clear paths for greater growth. Likewise, the perfect storm of signs which Jesus reveals to us also serve to clear a path for greater growth. The type of growth isn't just for the planet or for individual people, communities, states and nations, but for God's eternal kingdom.

Let's unpack this:

In Matthew 24, Mark 13 and Luke 21, Jesus gives us many of the global signs that will happen to let us know that His return to earth is drawing near. They are, increased deception, pestilence/plagues/pandemics, earthquakes, wars and rumors of wars, ethnic strife, Jewish and Christian persecution, raging oceanic events, atmospheric and interstellar phenomena. Jesus says these things are like birth pains (they will increase in intensity and frequency over time). He also says in reference to these signs, that they are not The End—but rather a prelude.

However, Jesus does reveal one SPECIFIC sign which He says will herald The End. Do you know what it is? We've already looked at the 6 signs in chapter 1. Here is the 7th sign which should give you hope and excitement. It is the GREATEST sign which indicates Jesus' return is closer than we realize. In Matthew 24:14, Jesus says:

*"And **this gospel of the kingdom** will be preached in the whole world as a testimony to all nations, and then the end will come."* (Emphasis mine.)

Jesus reveals that **before** The End will come, **the good news** about His eternal Kingdom must be preached to the entire world as a testimony to all nations. Here is our hope! All of the nations of the world **must** hear about Jesus! He gave that responsibility to His Church. Just think about that for a moment. Even while the 6 other signs are converging into a fear-inducing storm, there is a 7th sign which is ALSO happening: the gospel is spreading! And perhaps, a central purpose for God allowing the 6 other signs will be to open the hearts and minds of unbelievers so they will receive the gospel when they are presented with it! After all, our lives on earth are temporary. But what happens after we die—good or bad—that's for eternity!

So, what is the good news of the kingdom? Do we know it fully?

John 3:16-21 tells us the good news:

*"**16** For God so loved the world that he gave his one and only Son, that whoever believes in him shall not perish but have eternal life. **17** For God did not send his Son into the world to condemn the world, but to save the world through him. **18** Whoever believes in him is not condemned, but whoever does not believe stands condemned already because they have not believed in the name of God's one and only Son. **19** This is the verdict: Light has come into the world, but people loved darkness instead of light because their deeds were evil. **20** Everyone who does evil hates the light, and will not come into the light for fear that their deeds will be exposed. **21** But whoever lives by the truth comes into the light, so that it may be seen plainly that what they have done has been done in the sight of God."*

The good news is also found in John 3:3-8:

*"**3** Jesus replied, "Very truly I tell you, no one can see the kingdom of God unless they are born again." **4** "How can someone be born when they are old?" Nicodemus asked. "Surely they cannot enter a second time into their mother's womb to be born!" **5** Jesus answered, "Very truly I tell you, no one can enter the kingdom of God unless they are born of water and the Spirit. **6** Flesh gives birth to flesh, but the Spirit gives birth to spirit. **7** You should not be surprised at my saying, 'You must be born again.' **8** The wind blows wherever it pleases. You hear its sound, but you cannot tell where it comes from or where it is going. So it is with everyone born of the Spirit."*

It is also Romans 6:23:

*"**23** For the wages of sin is death, but the gift of God is eternal life in Christ Jesus our Lord."*

It is Acts 1:6-11:

*"**6** Then they gathered around him and asked him, "Lord, are you at this time going to restore the kingdom to Israel?" **7** He said to them: "It is not for you to know the times or dates the Father has set by his own authority. **8** But you*

will receive power when the Holy Spirit comes on you; and you will be my witnesses in Jerusalem, and in all Judea and Samaria, and to the ends of the earth." **9** *After he said this, he was taken up before their very eyes, and a cloud hid him from their sight.* **10** *They were looking intently up into the sky as he was going, when suddenly two men dressed in white stood beside them.* **11** *"Men of Galilee," they said, "why do you stand here looking into the sky? This same Jesus, who has been taken from you into heaven, will come back in the same way you have seen him go into heaven."* (Emphasis mine.)

It is Luke 24:44-47:

44 *He said to them, "This is what I told you while I was still with you: Everything must be fulfilled that is written about me in the Law of Moses, the Prophets and the Psalms."* **45** *Then he opened their minds so they could understand the Scriptures.* **46** *He told them, "This is what is written: The Messiah will suffer and rise from the dead on the third day,* **47** *and repentance for the forgiveness of sins will be preached in his name to all nations, beginning at Jerusalem.* **48** *You are witnesses of these things.* (Emphasis mine.)

It is Matthew 28:18-20:

*"***18** *Then Jesus came to them and said, "All authority in heaven and on earth has been given to me.* **19** *Therefore go and make disciples of all nations, baptizing them in the name of the Father and of the Son and of the Holy Spirit,* **20** *and teaching them to obey everything I have commanded you. And surely I am with you always, to the very end of the age."* (Emphasis mine.)

It is Matthew 24:29-31:

29 *"Immediately after the distress of those days "'the sun will be darkened, and the moon will not give its light; the stars will fall from the sky, and the heavenly bodies will be shaken.'* **30** *"Then will appear the sign of the Son of Man in heaven. And then all the peoples of the earth will mourn when they see the Son of Man coming on the clouds of heaven, with power and great glory.* **31** *And he will send his angels with a loud trumpet call, and they will gather his elect from the four winds, from one end of the heavens to the other."*[1] (Emphasis mine.)

It is Matthew 25:31-46:

31 *"When the Son of Man comes in his glory, and all the angels with him, he will sit on his glorious throne.* **32** *All the nations will be gathered before him, and he will separate the people one from another as a shepherd separates the sheep from the goats.* **33** *He will put the sheep on his right and the goats on his left.*

34 *"Then the King will say to those on his right, 'Come, you who are blessed by my Father; take your inheritance, the kingdom prepared for you since the creation of the world.* **35** *For I was hungry and you gave me something to eat, I was thirsty and you gave me something to drink, I was a stranger and you invited me in,* **36** *I needed clothes and you clothed me, I was sick and you looked after me, I was in prison and you came to visit me.'*

37 *"Then the righteous will answer him, 'Lord, when did we see you hungry and feed you, or thirsty and give you something to drink?* **38** *When did we see you a stranger and invite you in, or needing clothes and clothe you?* **39** *When did we see you sick or in prison and go to visit you?'*

40 *"The King will reply, 'Truly I tell you, whatever you did for one of the least of these brothers and sisters of mine, you did for me.'*

41 *"Then he will say to those on his left, 'Depart from me, you who are cursed, into the eternal fire prepared for the devil and his angels.* **42** *For I was hungry and you gave me nothing to eat, I was thirsty and you gave me nothing to drink,* **43** *I was a stranger and you did not invite me in, I needed clothes and you did not clothe me, I was sick and in prison and you did not look after me.'*

44 *"They also will answer, 'Lord, when did we see you hungry or thirsty or a stranger or needing clothes or sick or in prison, and did not help you?'* **45** *"He will reply, 'Truly I tell you, whatever you did not do for one of the least of these, you did not do for me.'*

46 *"Then they will go away to eternal punishment, but the righteous to eternal life."* (Emphasis mine.)

These passages present us with the crux of, **"this gospel of the kingdom."** These Scriptures represent the primary framework of the gospel. That humanity, though originally created good, is now fallen and in need of a Savior. That God the Father sent His Son, Jesus as our Savior and Lord. He took our punishment and died on the cross at Calvary.... But He didn't stay dead! He rose from the grave on the 3rd day with all power in His hands! He conquered death so that death would not have the last word on us!

He is now seated back in heaven with His Heavenly Father. But, that's not all! One day, He will physically return to earth as the KING of Kings and LORD of Lords! He will vanquish sin and evil, reward the righteous, usher in His eternal kingdom and bring restoration to all creation! There are many other Scripture passages that could be added to this list. However, these sum up the gospel of God's Kingdom, which Jesus says must be preached to the entire world before the events of the end of this Age will unfold. And He calls all who love and follow Him to participate with Him in His plan of salvation by sharing "this gospel of the kingdom" with others.

THE FINAL GENERATION?

In reference to all the signs Jesus told us to watch for, many have asked, are we the final generation? Are we the generation which will witness the return of Christ? Or will life continue on as it always has, without much change? Again, Jesus gives us the GREATEST sign to watch for: the spread of the gospel to the entire world...

Thanks to technology which has multiplied missionary efforts, our generation is the first and only one to be extremely close to achieving this reality of reaching the entire world with the gospel.

The gospel has been proclaimed everywhere except in one set of places that has been called, "The 10/40 window." There are approximately 2.5 billion people in this "window," which consists of North Africa and parts of the Middle East and Asia, who have not yet heard the gospel of God's Kingdom.[2]

If the stats are right, as numerous Christian organizations and churches have partnered to reach this area, this milestone could be achieved by or near 2030.[3]

If they are successful, at that point, all the nations of the world will have heard the gospel. Jesus says, when this happens then the events of The End will finally unfold. So, it looks like we may very well be the final generation before this chapter of human history concludes and a new chapter begins.

The Bible indicates that The End, also called "The Day of The LORD" consists of a series of climatic events which culminates with Jesus' world-wide return to earth to usher in His eternal kingdom.[4] Will you be ready for that day when He parts the sky and every eye sees Him?

WHAT DO WE DO?

So, what do we do? Jesus tells us. "When you see these things, look up, for your redemption draws near." Jesus tells us to not be afraid, even though we are surrounded by all of these signs. How is that possible? Well, in a hurricane, as destruction swirls all around… there is also a place of peace and safety… **that place is found in the eye of the storm**. We must maintain our connection to Jesus through His Word, prayer, worship and fellowship. If we see Him as He declares Himself to be: The True Vine, and we see ourselves as He says we are: Branches, then we will learn how to abide in Him. We will learn how to remain connected to Him. When we do, His overwhelming peace will secure us as the storm blows all around us. Jesus told us about all of these signs, so when we see and experience them, we would not be afraid. He has told us ahead of time so we would place our faith and trust in Him.[5]

We follow the One who slept soundly during a raging storm. We serve the One who stood in the face of raging winds and roaring waves and commanded: "Peace be still" and they obeyed![6] During this Perfect Storm which rages all around us and will increase in the coming years, Jesus is not speaking to the storm—because it will do what God has determined for it to do. Instead, Jesus is saying "peace be still" to our hearts. We do not have to remain afraid by what we see and experience.

The signs are all around us! The majority of them are happening at scales that are out of our control. However, the GREATEST sign, spreading the gospel to all nations, THAT is the one we can partner with God on! We can walk in the peace of God—in the Eye of the Storm—and be about our Father's business. That business is to live out and share the gospel so those who don't know Christ, can come to Him and those who already know Christ, can grow in Him.

Our Bridegroom is coming! May we see the Perfect Storm for what it truly is: a wake up call for the world. It is an invitation to humanity to come to the Savior while we still have time. The End of the Age is coming... the Bible tells us dark times are ahead. But it is the darkest nights when the light shines brightest! With every ending comes a new beginning. The ultimate end will bring the greatest beginning!

CHAPTER 4

WEATHERING THE STORM

Is all of this really happening? We've been looking at the "Biblical Weather Forecast" for the future of humanity and planet earth. We have examined several major signs which are converging on humanity to create The Perfect Storm. You may know others who are in denial of this inconvenient truth. They don't want to believe that one day life will change. Perhaps, before you began reading this book, you were in denial of this reality. But the facts are all present... swirling around us at this very moment. A storm is coming. So, the question is: **How do we weather this storm?** Throughout this book, I have provided suggestions to help you prepare for the storm. As we begin drawing this to a close, I want to focus on what Jesus says about how to weather any storm we may face in life.

Jesus states the following parable in Matthew 7:24-27:

24 *"Therefore everyone who hears these words of mine and puts them into practice is like a wise man who built his house on the rock.* **25** *The rain came down, the streams rose, and the winds blew and beat against that house; yet it did not fall, because it had its foundation on the rock.* **26** *But everyone who hears these words of mine and does not put them into practice is like a foolish man who built his house on sand.* **27** *The rain came down, the streams rose, and the winds blew and beat against that house, and it fell with a great crash."*

Two men are mentioned here in this story. One man is wise. The other is foolish. Both men represent humanity. The wise man represents those people who are spiritually wise. The foolish man represents those people who are spiritually foolish. The determination as to whether we are wise or foolish is based on how we treat the teachings of Christ. Both groups of people hear the teachings, but only one group actually *believes* His teachings and puts them into practice.

Both of these men built a house. The *houses* they built, represent their lives—the totality of their human existence. The wise man builds his life on the foundational rock of Jesus and His teachings. The foolish man builds his life on a foundation made of sand *(any other teaching, philosophy, ideology that can be found in the world apart from Christ).*

Notice that the same storm hits both men! The wise and the foolish (all people) will find themselves caught in the same storms of life! Torrential rain falls from the sky which causes massive flooding to take place! The storm also produces Hurricane-level winds which blow and beat against each person! However, those who have a solid foundation, are able to endure, survive and even thrive through the storm. Sadly, those whose foundation is sand, which shifts under the raging elements, fall apart and come to ruin.

DOOMSDAY PREPPERS

There are many non-Christians who are making physical preparations because they see the signs of the coming storm. They are building bunkers and gathering food, water, medical supplies, armaments and other resources. Their plan is to "ride out" the storm. They are busy fortifying their physical possessions in order to minimize the loss of loved ones and property. Now, I am all for taking precautions like this. It makes good common sense to have food, water, and medical supplies, stored up in case of major emergencies. Any way you can "harden" your home to help ensure your survival during storms, disasters, looting, etc., is a good thing! Not only does it make good common sense, but it also makes good biblical sense. Read Genesis 6-9 and you will see that God told Noah to become a "Doomsday Prepper." So, we should be physically prepared for the storms of life.

However, Jesus wants us to be more than physically prepared. The truth He offers, if we will listen and put it into action, will help us to be spiritually, mentally and emotionally prepared for the storms of life. He tells us the wise person will see the value in what He has to say, will then listen to Him, follow His teachings and become internally fortified against the storms of life. The foolish person, will only focus on their exterior life. This kind of focus only builds on sand and will lead to our destruction. While physical preparation is important, what is even more valuable is the spiritual, mental and emotional preparation that comes from being in a right relationship with our Heavenly Father through Christ.

THE ULTIMATE PREPARATION

So, how do we weather the perfect storm that is fast approaching? We focus on Jesus and His Word. We seek to know Jesus through His Word. We determine to follow Jesus by obeying His Word. In doing so, He has promised to sustain us.

In Revelation 3:10 the resurrected and glorified Jesus reveals there is an "hour of trial" that will come to test the inhabitants of the entire world. In Matthew 24:21, Jesus tells us this timeframe will be the worst in all of human history: *"For then there will be great distress, unequaled from the beginning of the world until now—and never to be equaled again."*

This is the culmination of the Perfect Storm: all of the strands of converging signs lead to the rise of the Antichrist and the worst time in human history. Even so, that does not negate Jesus' teachings. After all, Jesus taught that the Antichrist would come. So, if these signs are converging, as Jesus said they would, then also true, are His teachings which encourage us to build our lives on Truth! Jesus is the only way we will be able to endure, survive and thrive during the coming perfect storm!

So, how do we weather the coming storm? We focus on, listen to and obey Jesus. We study His Word. We put it into practice in our own lives. We ask Him to lead us in how to warn others and physically prepare for what's coming. We ask Him to empower us to walk in the peace, power and joy of His Holy Spirit. Yes, I said "joy." You may think, how does "joy" go with everything else? The second half of

Nehemiah 8:10 says, "Do not grieve, for the joy of the LORD is your strength."

The people of Israel had been ignorant of God's Word. In Nehemiah 8, the Word was read in their hearing and they began to weep. But, as the Word of God was explained to them, they were told to take refuge in it... to receive His joy as their strength! God's Word enables us to see reality for what it is and to see God for who He is. When we are able to truly see God and recognize His nearness to us—as He desires for us to do—then our response to outside negative circumstances will change. We will be able to walk in true spiritual resilience! Finding our joy in Christ, leads to us receiving His presence and power in order to face any situation that comes our way!

ONE BODY IN CHRIST

This brings us to an important truth. The Bible is clear that as the world draws closer to Jesus' return, the antichrist system will encourage unbelievers to persecute ALL of God's people. Persecution will not be based on nationality or ethnicity. It will be based on our Common Denominator: JESUS. Jesus says in John 15:18-19: *"**18** "If the world hates you, keep in mind that it hated me first. **19** If you belonged to the world, it would love you as its own. As it is, you do not belong to the world, but I have chosen you out of the world. That is why the world hates you."*

According to statistics,[1] globally, over 380 million Christians are being persecuted for their faith in Jesus. Our sisters and brothers in Christ are being ostracized from their families and communities, imprisoned and martyred. This persecution is on the rise and is sweeping across the planet. Soon it will be prevalent on American shores, as it is already making its way across other Western countries.

Persecution is coming for ALL Christians. Therefore, we need to unify together across denominational and ethnic lines now because we will need each other in the future.

JESUS' PEACE

Jesus makes us a promise in John 14:27: *"Peace I leave with you; my peace I give you. I do not give to you as the world gives. Do not let your hearts be troubled and do not be afraid."*

Let that sink in for a moment...

Jesus wants to give you and I a kind of peace that the storms of life can't touch! He wants to give us a peace which the fallen world system cannot provide! Jesus wants to give us is HIS OWN PEACE! Do you think for one moment that HIS PEACE is determined by how situations and circumstances play out on earth? Not at all.

HIS PEACE is determined by being in direct relationship with HIS HEAVENLY FATHER. As, I pointed out previously, Jesus was asleep in a boat during a storm while his disciples were filled with fear and anxiety. When they woke Him up, He was still at peace. When He spoke to the storm, He was at peace. When the storm died down, He was at peace. He then asked His disciples why they were not at peace. He asked why they did not have faith that because they were with Him, they would be alright?

Jesus wants to give us the same peace Jesus has! This is a staggering revelation! This is also the only way we will be able to weather the coming storm. We must realize that God is the One who holds our lives in His hands. And if we are in Christ, our eternal destiny is secure! So, we will be able to weather any storm because we are in direct relationship with the One who speaks peace to our souls. He will also speak peace to the coming storm, ***after*** it has accomplished the purposes for which God allowed it to be created.

So, be encouraged! If you keep Jesus as your primary focus and follow His leading, you will be able to weather the storm! And when all is said and done, you will hear God say, "Well done, my good and faithful servant." AMEN.

CHAPTER 5
AFTER THE STORM

The Bible tells us that the perfect storm is coming upon humanity. It will happen on a global scale. It will be the worst time in all of human history. God will give a rebellious humanity—which has sought to deny Him at every turn—over to itself. He will remove the restraints and allow the man of lawlessness to be fully welcomed and embraced by earth's inhabitants. The results of this storm will be horrific.

If our eyes are open, we can see the converging elements coming together even now. However, the Bible doesn't only tell us about the storm… It also tells us what happens after the storm is over!

Yes, it will be the darkest time in human history; but it is always darkest before the dawn. Dawn will come! But it won't be the sun which illuminates *that day*. The Bible tells us that *that day*—which will be the greatest day in all of human history—will be illuminated by the SON of GOD: Jesus Christ Himself![1]

The storm will end when Jesus returns! Jesus Himself told us this in Matthew 24. Here is what He taught about the storm and how it ends:

15 *"So when you see standing in the holy place 'the abomination that causes desolation,' spoken of through the prophet Daniel—let the reader understand —* **16** *then let those who are in Judea flee to the mountains.* **17** *Let no one on the housetop go down to take anything out of the house.* **18** *Let no one in the field go back to get their cloak.***19** *How dreadful it will be in those days for pregnant women and nursing mothers!* **20** *Pray that your flight will not take place in winter or on the Sabbath.* **21** *For then there will be great distress, unequaled from the beginning of the world until now—and never to be equaled again.*

22 *"If those days had not been cut short, no one would survive, but for the sake of the elect those days will be shortened.* **23** *At that time if anyone says* *to you, 'Look, here is the Messiah!' or, 'There he is!' do not believe it.* **24** *For false messiahs and false prophets will appear and perform great signs and wonders to deceive, if possible, even the elect.* **25** *See, I have told you ahead of time.*

26 *"So if anyone tells you, 'There he is, out in the wilderness,' do not go out; or, 'Here he is, in the inner rooms,' do not believe it.* **27** *For as lightning that comes from the east is visible even in the west, so will be the coming of the Son of Man.* **28** *Wherever there is a carcass, there the vultures will gather.*

29 *"Immediately after the distress of those days 'the sun will be darkened, and the moon will not give its light; the stars will fall from the sky, and the heavenly bodies will be shaken.'*

30 *"Then will appear the sign of the Son of Man in heaven. And then all the peoples of the earth will mourn when they see the Son of Man coming on the clouds of heaven, with power and great glory.* **31** *And he will send his angels with a loud trumpet call, and they will gather his elect from the four winds, from one end of the heavens to the other."*

Just like an atmospheric storm does not go on forever, the Perfect Storm which will come upon humanity will not last forever. Jesus will return in a display of great glory that will eclipse the Sun! And every person alive on earth at that moment will witness His arrival. At that time, no one will question who is in charge of the universe. It will be evident to all that Jesus is the KING of Kings and the LORD of Lords!

The storm will end at the pre-ordained moment when God is ready to install His eternal kingdom on earth in all of its vast glory! When that time comes, the Antichrist and the false prophet will be thrown alive into the lake of fire and the dragon (Lucifer/Satan/the devil) will be cast into the abyss. The devil's global empire, which will have ruled the world for a timeframe of 3.5 years, will be demolished![2]

It is important for us to pause here for a moment. In Acts 1:6-11, Jesus and his disciples have a conversation; that's followed by an angelic revelation:

*"**6** Then they gathered around him and asked him, "Lord, are you at this time going to restore the kingdom to Israel?" **7** He said to them: "It is not for you to know the times or dates the Father has set by his own authority. **8** But you will receive power when the Holy Spirit comes on you; and you will be my witnesses in Jerusalem, and in all Judea and Samaria, and to the ends of the earth." **9** After he said this, he was taken up before their very eyes, and a cloud hid him from their sight. **10** They were looking intently up into the sky as he was going, when suddenly two men dressed in white stood beside them. **11** "Men of Galilee," they said, "why do you stand here looking into the sky? This same Jesus, who has been taken from you into heaven, will come back in the same way you have seen him go into heaven."*

Jesus spent 40 days with His disciples after his resurrection, during which He taught additional things about God's Kingdom. They asked Him about the fulfillment of the promises God made to Israel through the prophets—that the earthly kingdom would be restored to them. Notice, Jesus doesn't say it won't happen. <u>He says that the time of restoration has already been set for a future date by His Father</u>. In the meantime, their focus should be to bring as many people as possible into God's Kingdom.

The disciples expected Jesus to restore the Kingdom to Israel shortly after His resurrection. Jesus does not deny their expectation of restoration. He simply says, "the time for restoration is not yet" (*my paraphrase*). However, after the disciples watch Jesus ascend back to heaven, two angels appear and tell them one day Jesus will return again to that very spot! In the angels' statement rests the foreshadowing... If Jesus is the one who will restore the kingdom back to Israel, and He has just ascended to heaven, then logic dictates that the kingdom will be restored to Israel when Jesus returns to earth. This is exactly what the Bible teaches! **Let's continue...**

When Jesus returns, He will sit on His royal throne in Jerusalem and restore the kingdom to Israel. He will then judge the people of the nations based on whether they received Him and how they treated Israel. The righteous will be rewarded with entrance into His eternal kingdom. The wicked will be condemned to punishment in the eternal flames prepared for the devil and his angels. The crooked places will be made straight. Every arrogance will be made low. Injustice will finally be corrected. And God's people will shine like the stars in the heavens![3]

Let me stop here for a moment.

Perhaps the content of the above paragraph is new to you. In this time of rising antisemitism, who wants to hear that Jesus will return to earth and stand with the Jews? But this is exactly what the Scriptures tell us. Right now, as a nation, the Jews do not follow Jesus. However, by the time Jesus returns, they will have finally repented and turned back to Him. This is one of the main reasons for the Tribulation period. It is a time of testing for the Jews *first,* as well as for the rest of the world. It is the mechanism God will use to bring His people (Jew and Gentile) to repentance.

It's important for us to realize that when Jesus was incarnated into the world, through Mary, He was born *Jewish.* He lived as a *Jewish* man and followed the biblical traditions of the Old Testament. Hanging above His head at His crucifixion was a sign which read: "Jesus of Nazareth, The King of the Jews." After His bodily resurrection from the dead and physical ascension back into heaven, He now, sits at the right hand of His Heavenly Father—still being *Jewish.* In Revelation 5:5, He is called the "Lion of the tribe of Judah" and "the Root of David." These titles are distinctly *Jewish.*

Jesus has, in no way, divorced Himself from the Jews. For as the Scriptures testify, "salvation is of the Jews" and "the gospel is the power of God unto salvation to everyone who believes, first to the Jew, then to the Gentile." Jesus is—according to what's termed the Hypostatic Union—both God and Man. From a human standpoint, He is thoroughly Jewish and the rightful Savior of Israel AND the rest of the world. Jesus will stand with all persons—Jew and Gentile—who place their trust in Him.[4]

In his book, *When A Jew Rules the World: What the Bible Really Says About Israel in the Plan of God,* Joel Richardson says the following:

"According to Jesus, the destiny of nations in the Day of Judgment, whether they are cast away or welcomed into the kingdom of God, is largely contingent upon their treatment of His brethren. Jesus even went so far as to say that how the nations treated His brethren is how they treated Him. He deeply identifies with this people group, taking their mistreatment as His mistreatment. Surely determining the identity of who Jesus was referring to is absolutely crucial.

"Interpreters have suggested three different ways to understand this term. Some have argued that Jesus was speaking of the Jewish people, His actual blood "brethren." Others argue that Jesus was speaking about His disciples or anyone who willingly follows Jesus. Still others say that Jesus was simply referring to the poor, the suffering, and the oppressed in general. Now, while Christian care for the poor and the oppressed is certainly a central feature of the Christian faith, it is not what this passage is speaking about... When we see Matthew 25 in its actual full context, it becomes clear that when Jesus spoke of His "brethren," He was referring to the inhabitants of Jerusalem and Judea who will suffer during the time of "Jacob's distress," which He had just described in chapter 24.

"We must also recognize that when Jesus taught that the nations would be judged based on their mistreatment of Israel, in no way was He making a new point. The wrath of God executed against Israel's enemies at the Day of Judgement is a theme that is repeated many times throughout the Prophets."[5]

The Scriptures are clear. Israel still lies at the center of God's restoration plan for humanity, the planet and all creation! And when Jesus returns, Jerusalem, from which He will reign, will become the capital city of the planet. This reality is something for us to seriously consider, especially as a growing number of nations currently seek Israel's demise.

Let's continue...

Like a clean up that happens after an atmospheric storm, the greatest restoration of the earth will happen after the perfect storm has ended! Jesus calls it, The Renewal of all things...".[6] The apostle Paul talks about it as well in Romans 8, when the children of God are finally revealed with Christ and the creation, which was subjected to sinful corruption, will finally be liberated! Yes, the earth will be restored! Jesus will do it! And we who belong to Him will be invited to partner alongside Him in the work! And we will hear Him say to us: "Well done, good and faithful servant! You have been faithful with a few things; I will put you in charge of many things. Come and share your master's happiness!"[7]

When Jesus returns and restores the earth, the greatest family reunion in the universe will take place! God the Father will throw a banquet of celebration for His Son, who has triumphed over all evil and for us who are co-heirs—adopted into His family through Christ.[8] Then the prayer Jesus taught us to pray will finally be fully realized: "...Thy kingdom come, Thy will be done on earth as it is in Heaven..." After the storm, it will literally and finally be "heaven on earth!" Then all of God's people found in the Old and New Testaments, and from every generation throughout all of human history—from every tribe, people, language and nation will be gathered together. Billions of us who are the children of God and citizens of His glorious kingdom of light will forever be with the LORD!

God's original intent for humanity, the world and the universe will finally be fulfilled! The utopia we have always dreamed of, but have never been able to create due to our sin and wickedness, will finally be known and experienced! God Himself, who made provisions for a perfect creation in the very beginning will bring it to us![9]

Go to the end of the book and read the last four chapters of Revelation for yourself. Witness how the end of the storm takes place and how the brightest dawn unfolds thereafter. Read those chapters for yourself and believe!

The perfect storm will come. But, it serves to usher in the climactic return of JESUS: the King and Champion of Heaven and Earth!

CLOSING THOUGHTS

"...when the Son of Man comes, will he find faith on the earth?" — Jesus (Luke 18:8b)

What I have sought to offer in this book is factual information and not sensationalism. While some things have been speculative—like exactly how the image of the Beast will operate—I have sought to ground my speculation in the information we have available to us. There is much more which could be said on the subject matter presented in this book. However, my purpose is to present an overview of these issues in order to help you see the critical nature of where we are in history. You may find this book alarming. Or you may not. You may feel the temptation to be like an ostrich and stick your head in the sand. You may think, "Life will continue like it always has. I can just focus on my own agenda, dreams and goals."

But the truth is, life never continues indefinitely, "like it always has." Major shifts in society do come. These are like "BC/AD" moments. One day, things are the same and then a major event happens. From that moment on, every day afterward is completely different. Humanity is rapidly approaching the threshold of a seismic shift. The question is not, "If it will happen?" The question is, "When?"

I have had numerous conversations with fellow believers over the years. Many have told me they are praying for world peace. They are thinking there must be a way for the Church to provide a smooth transition between our current age and the Age to come. They look at the signs around us and believe the peace they are praying for can be realized without us having to go through traumatic global events. They believe that somehow the Church can help the world usher in utopia. Sadly, they misunderstand or are ignorant of what the Scriptures teach.

No matter how hard humanity works at trying to create an ideal utopia, the Bible is clear: all of our efforts will ultimately lead to a dystopian future. Why is this? **Because we are fallen, imperfect beings trying to create the perfect system without God.** History reveals that many countries have tried to create utopia. All have failed —often resulting in great bloodshed. Looking forward, the Bible reveals a future which cannot be stopped because humanity refuses to yield to God's truth. As many of the quotes in this book reveal, *we are determined to go our own way.*

Even though this is the case, God calls His people to represent Him! In Matthew 28 and Acts 1, we see that Jesus calls His Church to be His witnesses—stretching around the planet and across the generations, until the end of this age arrives and Jesus returns! For us today, this means His Church is called to represent Him during this crucial time in history. Where we stand today and in the future matters. It will prove to be the most difficult and yet the most impactful landscape!

Sadly, as the elements of this dystopian future converge all around us, the Church is fragmented. Many congregations are divided along ethnic and political lines. Many congregants are drowning in unforgiveness, in-fighting and pursuing their own agendas rather than the Agenda of Christ. Many church leaders view our present-day struggles through a worldly lens, rather than through the eternal reality of the Scriptures. They thus respond to these struggles just as unbelievers would and not how God says His children should.

The devil (and those he uses) wants the Church to remain divided and solely focused on the here-and-now. The enemy wants the Church distracted by issues of race, education, housing, politics, etc. Having only this emphasis blinds us to the larger global machinations which are being erected around us all. As Jesus said in Matthew 15:14, when the blind leads the blind, both fall into the ditch.

The Bible is clear that the coming Antichrist will **make war against the saints** and will prevail for a time.[1] All around us today, we can see the systems being erected to welcome his arrival. If a war is coming, we must seek the LORD to find out how He wants us to fight! The

Bible tells us in 2 Corinthians 10:4 that, *"the weapons of our warfare are not carnal, but are mighty to the pulling down of strongholds."* In other words, we are not limited to merely physical acts of strength and resistance in our efforts to stand against the coming tide. While we are not called to start wars, we ***are*** called to preserve the lives of the innocent and resist in ways that provide the enemies of God with an opportunity to see the error of their ways and repent. If they don't, then only God's judgment awaits them.

An entire globalist, transhumanist system is now coming together where we must depend almost 100% on digital technology and services. These are powered by artificial intelligence and are completely trackable and controllable by those who created them. At the same time, the radical adherents of Islam seek global dominance. While these things happen, deception and the occult continue to infiltrate our lives. And… there's the possibility that earth may be hit by the Apophis asteroid in 2029.

The perfect storm is coalescing and gaining strength! We have less time than we think. We must wake up and prepare so when Jesus returns we can be counted among His faithful servants who have not fallen away!

To help, here are 12 concrete steps we can take. You may not be able to put all of these into practice simultaneously; but, as you read this list make a decision to put 1-2 steps into practice as soon as possible. Then add additional steps over time.

ONE: We must begin to educate each other, through the lens of Scripture, on the various aspects of the Antichrist System which is rising before our eyes. This will enable us to think critically about the situation and begin to develop countermeasures. This includes understanding spiritual warfare in the midst of increasing occult activity and reducing our digital footprint and usage of smart-enabled devices. We've been conditioned to think all messages in entertainment are harmless and digital technology is our friend. But this can't be further from the truth. The Bible says we are to "test the spirits by the Spirit." We must be discerning! We should not be unaware of the devil's deceptive schemes.[2]

TWO: We must begin working to cross the ethnic divide *within* the Body of Christ, because the enemy is coming for us all. We will need each other's support and expertise. "A house divided against itself cannot stand."[3] We no longer have time to maintain a segregated Church. All ethnic groups within the Body of Christ must come together—black, white, asian, hispanic, etc... including our messianic Jewish brothers and sisters as well. Ephesians 4 tells us that our strength is found in unifying together around Jesus Christ.

THREE: We must begin creating our own networks (communication, food, health, land, skills, defense, etc), which exist outside of mainstream digital systems. This will require us to secure appropriate analogue communication devices that cannot be tracked and cannot be affected by tech outages. We will also need to implement underground church practices similar to what is used in places and times where Christianity has been/is outlawed. This needs to also include shelter-in-place, evacuation and defensive plans.

FOUR: We must live out and share the gospel with the lost (Jews & Gentiles), letting them know about Jesus' gift of salvation, the coming Antichrist System, Jesus' Return and final judgment. This includes ministering to the basic physical needs of those inside and outside the Church based on Matthew 25:31-46.

FIVE: We must pay attention to what happens in Israel and the Middle East. This is important because some in Christendom think Israel no longer matters. They believe God is done with national Israel and has "moved on" to the Church. This is an erroneous teaching called, Replacement Theology. There are, however, **many** scriptural passages throughout the Bible which clearly refute this line of thinking. One such example is Zechariah chapters 12 to 14, which speak of Christ rescuing the nation of Israel from the attacks of the world's nations at the end of the age. Why would Jesus do that if God has completely cast away the nation of Israel? [Also see Revelation 12 which is primarily about the nation of Israel during the Tribulation.]

Scripture indicates what happens in Israel and the Middle East serves as an indicator of where we are on God's End Times Timeline. This is not popular to say in our socio-political climate, but Israel's rebirth as a nation in 1948 is a clear sign for us to pay attention. God still has a purpose for the people, land and nation of Israel. It is built on the foundation of unconditional promises He gave in Genesis—which stretch to the end of Revelation. As Christians, we should be grateful God will keep His promises to Israel, because that shows He will also keep His promises to us. God's ways and thoughts are higher than ours. We must seek to align our thinking with His and not choose our limited understanding above His declared will.

SIX: We must prepare ourselves for the eventuality of suffering for Christ. Study the lives of Jesus followers, in the Bible and in past/current history. In many places in the world, our sisters and brothers in Christ are already being persecuted for their faith in Jesus.[4]

SEVEN: We must encourage each other to develop our spirit, soul and body. It is time for us to get in shape because when participation in the Antichrist System becomes mandatory, those who refuse the Mark must be in the best position to thrive outside of that System. So, develop a workout routine to grow your spirit, your mind (thoughts & emotions), and your bodily health and strength. (Also, being in your best shape helps in regular everyday settings too!)

EIGHT: We must encourage one another to "look up" and focus on Christ's Coming Kingdom. Our hope has to be placed firmly in Christ. While we are in this world, our allegiance cannot be to the fallen aspects of the world system. Our identity and our citizenship is to be found in Christ.

NINE: We must pray for our enemies. Jesus is **very** clear in Matthew 5:43-48 that we are to love and pray for our enemies. There is no way around His command. If we are going to be His disciples, we must act in prayerful and loving ways towards those who oppose God and His people. A central reason for this is because those humans we consider to be enemies, are not THE enemy. Satan is our True Enemy. By praying for and blessing our enemies, we open the door of possibility for them to see Jesus in our actions and receive Him into their lives.

TEN: We must prepare our hearts to see and experience miracles. Throughout the Bible, God has always miraculously provided for His people when they followed Him in faith. The last time I checked, we have not reached the end of the book of Revelation yet. This means we are STILL IN BIBLE DAYS! Hebrews 13:8 tells us that Jesus Christ is the same yesterday, today and forever. God is still doing miracles, even if we don't often see them where we live.

The purpose of miracles isn't just God meeting our needs, but even more so, miracles point us to God and help us build our faith in and on Christ. Do your research. There are many accounts of God performing bonafide miraculous interventions right in our day: bringing people back from the dead, healing broken bodies, protecting in the midst of clear and present danger, providing when all resources are gone![5] God desires to step into our situations in ways we can't even imagine. But we have to have our hearts and minds open to the possibility. With what is coming in the future, we will need to walk in the miraculous provision of God's kingdom.

ELEVEN: Pray for Muslims to surrender to Jesus! Fear is rising in America as its citizens are realizing the very real dangers of radical Islam. People are asking what they can do to combat the waves of attacks that have already begun. Let's take a look at what is happening on the other side of the world. Even now, while there is warfare happening between Israel and the surrounding Islamic nations, God has been working huge miracles!

The gospel is being preached to both Jews and Muslims and many are coming to faith in Jesus! The mainstream media is not talking about this, but reports are coming in through Christian networks and ministries with "boots on the ground" in these areas. Many Muslims are receiving visions of Jesus and are being led to Christians so they can hear the gospel message. Reports state that thousands of mosques have closed as up to one million Muslims have left Islam for a relationship with Jesus![6]

When I first wrote this section in November 2025, the Iranian regime was fighting to maintain its 45-year grip over the country. Many Muslim citizens had grown disillusioned with the oppressive leadership of their supreme leader, Ayatollah Ali Khamenei. According to CBN, an anonymous internal poll found that 80% of the Iranian population preferred democracy.[7] Then, a significant uprising began in late December and continued into 2026. The regime killed many thousands of its own citizens in an attempt to maintain control. Then, at the end of February, the U.S. and Israeli militaries intervened —striking down many key leaders of the regime—and Iranians all over the world celebrated.

Now, we find ourselves in a time of war and uncertainty… What will the outcome be? Time will tell. But what is clear, if one looks through a biblical lens[8], is that God is in control and He's on the move in the Middle East *(and around the world)*! Miracles are happening! Those who were enemies of Christ, Israel, America and the West are coming to the truth that is found in Jesus.

So, as the tide of Islam rises, let us pray that the same miracles that are now happening in the Middle East, will happen here! Let us pray that God will go before us and break the hearts of Muslims so they can be open to receive the true gospel of Jesus Christ!

TWELVE: Even with the various struggles and deceptive realities we have looked at in this book, God's command in 1 Thessalonians 5:16-18 still stands: ***16*** *"Rejoice always,* ***17*** *pray continually,****18*** *give thanks in all circumstances; for this is God's will for you in Christ Jesus."*

There is no **small print** that says, "if things don't work out how you like, you do not have to obey this Scripture passage." What God tells us to do, in this passage, is not based on any earthly circumstance we might encounter. Rather, we can "rejoice, pray and give thanks" because our focus is on the truth that God is SOVEREIGN! He is seated on His throne, ruling heaven and earth! His plans cannot be thwarted! That includes His plan for your life.

If Paul and Silas could sing praises to God while chained in a prison (Acts 16), surely we can worship the Lord through any storm we face!

The world is still full of God's glory—even if that glory is clouded by the sinful deeds of humanity. If you and I are born again then we have been given the ability to see the kingdom of God wherever we are—in every situation! Because of this, we can "rejoice, pray and give thanks." So, as you plan for the coming storm, include in your plans ways you can enjoy life! Still be creative and grow your skills and talents. Still dream, hope and imagine! After all, even though the thief comes to steal, kill and destroy, Jesus said He has come to give us abundant life![9] And He has called us to be salt and light![10]

MUST THESE THINGS HAPPEN?

The Bible is clear: these things must happen. All of the elements of The Perfect Storm mentioned in this book must come to pass. There is no stopping them. However, the Bible is also clear that Christ died to save the ungodly—those who are enemies against Him.[11] God is still saving people from every part of society—that includes those who are currently part of the negative elements that have been presented in this book.

So, may we become intentional about praying for the salvation of those who use deception and are involved in the occult. May we pray for the salvation of those who are developing Artificial Intelligence. May we pray for the salvation of those with globalist agendas. May we pray for the salvation of the transhumanists who are too afraid to trust God and would rather create their own idol. May we pray for the Islamic Militant Extremists who want to watch Western civilization burn. And may we pray for the astronomers, scientists, and officials who may be hiding information about the coming asteroid from the public.

Everyone in these groups won't get saved. But perhaps, through prayer, quite a few will receive Jesus Christ as their Lord and Savior! The truth of the matter is, while they may be enemies, they are not

THE enemy. Satan is humankind's ultimate enemy who will manipulate and destroy anyone he can get his hands on.

Ephesians 3:20 tells us that God is able to do exceedingly, abundantly above all we can ask or think, according to the power that is at work in us. So, may we partner with the Holy Spirit and allow His Power to work in us… as we intentionally pray for our enemies.

AM I OVERREACTING?

A pastor told me I was overreacting… That yes, we are in the Last Days, but that the tribulation was probably hundreds, if not thousands of years away. Part of me hopes I am overreacting to what is happening in the world. I would love to just live my life as if nothing is wrong.

I would love to believe him. After all, who wants to go through a time of immense suffering? But there are too many "coincidences" between prophetic Scripture and actual happenings. The fallen world system is conditioning the global population for a coming regime change. The elites aren't even hiding it anymore. They are now upfront about their globalist agenda to usher in a new world order. At the same time, radical Islamists are vocal about conquering the West and the world. Fortunately for us, God told us about this ahead of time in His Word.

But will we listen and govern ourselves accordingly? Or will we dismiss this warning as just another example of the Church crying wolf (and the wolf, once again is not there)? If you remember the story of the Boy Who Cried Wolf, at some point the wolf *actually* did show up. The Church, down through history has cried "wolf" many times when it came to the technology that would give rise to Mark of the Beast. We claimed the Mark was the social security number. Then it was barcodes. Then it was credit cards. And so on. And each time we cried wolf, people reacted, only to find that we were incorrect. Now, as the cry goes out, many may refuse to respond. But we seem to be very close to the time when the wolf is actually at the door!

I would rather we, as the Body of Christ, be prepared for what may come, than be unprepared when it finally does come. In this book we've examined societal indicators—from the increase of deception and the occult; to the rise of the Internet, artificial intelligence and the surveillance state; to the advancement of globalist agendas; to the prevalence of Transhumanism; to the expansion of Islamist extremism; to the coming Apophis asteroid; and the spread of the gospel to all nations. There's also the things we haven't covered which are usually mentioned when talking about the end times: wars, rumors of wars, and natural disasters.

All of these indicate that the Age in which we now live is drawing to a close. If this is in fact the case, then the next major event on God's Last Days Timeline will be the 7 year Tribulation. This will usher in the global Antichrist System, and the Antichrist himself. And it will end with, The Day of The LORD—God's outpouring of wrath on earth's unbelieving population followed by the global return of Christ!

Time will tell how long before these things happen. They could happen within our lifetime or the lifetime of our children and grandchildren. Either way… we need to prepare. May we have eyes to see what God is up to and ears to hear what the Holy Spirit is saying to the Church! The enemy may be using unbelievers to create a storm to deceive the masses, but according to Jeremiah 30, God has created a storm of His own to destroy the enemy and those who side with him:

23 "See, the storm of the Lord will burst out in wrath, a driving wind swirling down on the heads of the wicked. 24 The fierce anger of the Lord will not turn back until he fully accomplishes the purposes of his heart. In days to come you will understand this."

May we remember: God is sovereign. He is in control and is working everything according to the counsel of His will. The Scriptures bear this out. His Word can be trusted! As I close this book, I thought it is only fitting that we end with the powerful hymn, written in 1834 by Edward Mote. My prayer is that it becomes our bold declaration.

1 My hope is built on nothing less than Jesus' blood and righteousness; I dare not trust the sweetest frame, but wholly lean on Jesus' name.

Refrain: On Christ, the solid Rock, I stand: all other ground is sinking sand; all other ground is sinking sand.
2 When darkness veils His lovely face, I rest on His unchanging grace; in every high and stormy gale, my anchor holds within the veil.

Refrain: On Christ, the solid Rock, I stand: all other ground is sinking sand; all other ground is sinking sand.

3 His oath, His covenant, His blood, support me in the whelming flood; when all around my soul gives way, He then is all my hope and stay.

Refrain: On Christ, the solid Rock, I stand: all other ground is sinking sand; all other ground is sinking sand.

4 When He shall come with trumpet sound, O may I then in Him be found: dressed in His righteousness alone, faultless to stand before the throne.

Refrain: On Christ, the solid Rock, I stand: all other ground is sinking sand; all other ground is sinking sand.

When Jesus comes, will He find faith on the earth? Will He find those who still believe and trust Him even though they face tremendous opposition? May our answer be a resounding YES! By the grace and mercy of God, may we be salt and light in these darkening times. May others see our good works and glorify our Father in heaven. **Maranatha: Come Lord Jesus, come!**

AFTERWORD

Thank you for reading this book! I do have a request before you put it down (or turn off your e-reader). If you have found this book to be a blessing and an informative resource: **Please consider taking a few minutes to write a short review on Amazon and/or Goodreads.**

As an independent author, I rely on "word of mouth" more than any other promotional tools to help spread the word about my books. Your review means a lot to me and helps others make an informed decision about purchasing this work.

If this book has impacted you on a deep level—*perhaps even challenging you in some good and unexpected ways*—consider going beyond leaving a review. **Feel free to post about this book on your social media and/or purchase copies for family, friends, members of your faith community and book clubs.**

If you *really* feel ambitious and want to do even more to help this message spread to more Christ-followers, **reach out to your church leaders to plan an author visit.** I am always willing to present the information in this book to groups within the body of Christ.

Finally, this book has been a labor of love—for Christ and His Church. I have committed a considerable amount of time, effort and prayer into writing this for the purpose of helping God's people prepare for His Return. The world moves at breakneck speed with new developments happening almost daily. My prayer is that this book will provide a foundational framework and lens to help you stand firm and see through any deception of the enemy. So, use this book as a springboard to dive into your Bible! Pray for the Holy Spirit's guidance as you search the Scriptures—like the Bereans of Acts 17—to see if these things are true. May the sovereign love of God carry you in His purposes during this most crucial time in human history, as you seek to be a faithful witness unto Jesus.

—Allen Paul Weaver III

NOTES

Introduction: *A Wake-up Call*

1. 2 Thessalonians 2:1-12; 2 Timothy 3:2-5; 1 Timothy 4:1-2; Ephesians 2:1-3
2. Daniel 7; Revelation 13

Chapter 1: *The End Times Convergence of 6 Significant Happenings*

1. 1 John 8:32
2. The 2019 Brazil Carnival parade had a performance where a performer who was dressed like the devil attacked and defeated another performer representing Jesus. This scene caused controversy among religious groups. The 2024 Paris Olympics opening ceremony received international backlash for a segment that mocked The Last Supper (where Jesus ate with His disciples). The opening segment featured drag queens, transgendered persons and a blue-painted man representing the Greek god Dionysus.
3. Isaiah 5:20
4. Lennox, God, AI & The End of History, p.353-354
5. NPR.org article title: "We asked clergy if they use AI to help write sermons. Here's what they said." Article link: https://www.npr.org/2025/07/17/nx-s1-5468637/clergy-grapple-with-the-ethics-of-using-ai-to-write-sermons
6. In June 2023, a lutheran church in Fuerth, Bavaria hosted a 40-minute, AI-led service. ChatGPT was used to create 98% of the content, including the sermon, prayers and music. Four different digital avatars lead the service on a large screen. The service attracted over 300 attendees.

   In September 2023, Violet Crown City Church in Austin, Texas produced an experimental service that was entirely created by ChatGPT: liturgy, prayers, original music and sermon.

In March 2025, St. Paul's Lutheran Church in Helsinki, Finland held a service that was mostly created by Artificial Intelligence. AI tools wrote the sermon, several songs, composed music, created the visuals and a dialogue between Jesus and Satan. Over 120 people attended.

7. In 2019, an AI robot named Mindar (goddess of mercy), began delivering ancient Buddhist teachings and interacting with worshippers at the Kodai-ji Buddhist temple in Kyoto, Japan.

8. An Internet search reveals that growing numbers of people are using AI chatbots as replacements for human interaction.

9. Website of the AI app that enables the creation of digital avatar chatbots, including those of deceased loved ones: 2wai.ai

10. BBC.com article: "'A Predator in Your Home': Mothers say chatbots encouraged their sons to kill themselves". Link: https://www.bbc.com/news/articles/ce3xgwyywe4o

    ABCnews.go.com article: "AI chatbot dangers: Are there enough guardrails to protect children and other vulnerable people?"

    Link: https://abcnews.go.com/Technology/chatbot-dangers-guardrails-protect-children-vulnerable-people story?id=127099944

11. AI Chatbot Psychosis is defined as: a phenomenon where individuals reportedly develop or experience worsening cases of paranoia and delusions in connection with their use of chatbots. In these cases, the chatbots reinforce and amplify delusional thinking.

    Psychology Today article: "The Emerging Problem of 'AI Psychosis: Amplifications of delusions by AI chatbots may be worsening breaks with reality'"

    Link: https://www.psychologytoday.com/us/blog/urban-survival/202507/the-emerging-problem-of-ai-psychosis

12. A 2025 U.S. Senate report—"Big Tech Oligarchs' War Against Workers"—warned that Artificial Intelligence, automation and robotics could displace nearly 100 million jobs over the next decade.

13. In 2024, Elon Musk's AI company, xAI, built the "Colossus" supercomputer facility in Memphis, TN. It is the world's most powerful AI training center. Temporary gas turbines were used to power the massive facility. The turbine emissions has caused serious air pollution issues for local residents.

    CBS News' "60 Minutes Overtime" produced an exposé called: "Kenyan workers with AI jobs thought they had tickets to the future until the grim reality set in." It was revealed that big AI companies are exploiting data workers in Kenya (India, the Philippines and Venezuela) who train AI's large language models. Workers are being overworked, underpaid and treated badly. Nor are they receiving the mental health support they need to deal with the countless hours of cataloguing gratuitous negative imagery and video content for the AI systems.

    Article Link: https://www.cbsnews.com/news/ai-work-kenya-exploitation-60-minutes/

14. Even with more than 30k signatures, including from various notable individuals, the Future of Life Institute's open letter—Pause Giant AI Experiments: *We call on all AI labs to immediately pause for at least 6 months the training of AI systems more powerful than GPT-4"* —had little effect on global AI development.

    Link: https://futureoflife.org/open-letter/pause-giant-ai-experiments/

15. Tegmark, LIFE 3.0: Being Human in the Age of Artificial Intelligence, p.36-37

16. You can do a simple Google search for more information on the development of AlphaGo and AlphaGo Zero. But here are two Wikipedia links and a link to the video documentary.

    Link for AlphaGo: https://en.wikipedia.org/wiki/AlphaGo

Link for AlphaGo Zero: https://en.wikipedia.org/wiki/AlphaGo_Zero

You can watch the YouTube documentary produced by Google DeepMind and Reel As Dirt. It's called, AlphaGo — The Movie.

17. Dr. Ben Goertzel has been at the forefront of cutting edge Artificial Intelligence development for decades. There are hundreds of hours of interviews with him all over the Internet. You can search for and watch his 16 minute April 23, 2019 TEDxBerkeley Talk on the YouTube channel: Tedx Talks, to gain an overview of his beliefs and work as mentioned in this book. He basically plots out the trajectory of AI development. Here we are in 2026 and things are happening in line with what he said.

18. Do a Google search on "how AI is changing the way we think and perceive the world." There is a wealth of information which delve into this topic. One fundamental aspect is that we are moving from active mental searching and critical thinking to allowing AI to find our information and make decisions for us.

19. Ray Kurzweil has made comments about creating a digital god in multiple videos and documentaries, many which can be found on YouTube. He believes in exponential growth of technology and information, which will make creating a digital god possible.

20. Although the Way of the Future Church (WOTF), founded by Anthony Levandowski is currently defunct, the AI worship movement continues as increasing numbers of people view AI as an emergent digital god. Another web-based religious AI group is: ChurchofAI.us

21. Bar, god of A.I.: The Deification of Artificial Intelligence and the Rise of a New Technomancy Religion, p.66

22. Sampson, Revelation Now: Viewing the Tragedies and Triumph of Believers—Building Faith for Life Now, p.31

23. Harari, Homo Deus: A Brief History of Tomorrow, p. 22-23

24. Harari, p.24, 28

25. Harari, p. 49

26. Jewish Persecution: https://jcfa.org/article/the-expulsion-of-the-jews-from-muslim-countries-1920-1970-a-history-of-ongoing-cruelty-and-discrimination/

    The 1988 Hamas Charter shows radical Islam's full commitment to the destruction of the Jews (first), Christians and any non-muslim nation that will not submit to Islam: https://avalon.law.yale.edu/21st_century/hamas.asp

    Christian Persecution: OpenDoorsUS.org / Persecution.com / https://en.wikipedia.org/wiki/Persecution_of_Christians_by_the_Islamic_State

27. https://isgap.org/post/2025/06/canada-faces-rising-national-security-risk-from-muslim-brotherhood-infiltration-report-warns/

    PBS Frontline Article — "Crossing Boarders: How Terrorists Use Fake Passports, Visas and Other Identity Documents" Website: https://www.pbs.org/wgbh/pages/frontline/shows/trail/etc/fake.html

    PBS Frontline Article — "The Evolution of Islamic Terrorism" Website: https://www.pbs.org/wgbh/pages/frontline/shows/target/etc/modern.html

    Institute for Strategic Dialogue Article: "Twenty Years On: Assessing the UK Islamist Terrorism Landscape Since 7/7" Website: https://www.isdglobal.org/digital-dispatch/twenty-years-on-assessing-the-uk-islamist-terrorism-landscape-since-7-7/

    George Washington University Article: "Jihad Transformed: The Australian Experience of Islamic State Terrorism and Extremism" Website: https://extremism.gwu.edu/australia-and-islamic-state-terrorism-and-extremism

FBI Law Enforcement Bulletin: "Radicalization of Islamist Terrorists in the Western World" Website: https://leb.fbi.gov/articles/perspective/perspective-radicalization-of-islamist-terrorists-in-the-western-world

28. George Washington University, Program on Extremism, "The Muslim Brotherhood in America: A Brief History" (2025), Lorenzo Vindino, p.19-26 Website: https://extremism.gwu.edu/sites/g/files/zaxdzs5746/files/2025-07/The Muslim Brotherhood in America.pdf

Hoover Institution, "The Challenge of Dawa: Political Islam as Ideology and Movement and How to Counter It" (2017), Ayaan Hirsi Ali, p.20-21 Website: https://www.hoover.org/sites/default/files/research/docs/ali_challengeofdawa_final_web.pdf

29. The Muslim Brotherhood in America: A Brief History, 2025, Lorenzo Vindino, p. 31

30. The Challenge of Dawa: Political Islam as Ideology and Movement and How to Counter It, 2017, Ayaan Hirsi Ali, p.36, Glossary of Terms

31. The Muslim Brotherhood in America: A Brief History, 2025, Lorenzo Vindino, p. 11

32. The Challenge of Dawa: Political Islam as Ideology and Movement and How to Counter It, 2017, Ayaan Hirsi Ali, p.10, 19, 21, 42

33. Cahn, The Dragon's Prophecy: Israel, the Dark Resurrection and the End of Days, chapter 53

34. Pastor Josh Howerton talks about a connection between Galatians 1:8 and Revelation 20:4 and Islam. Checkout the YouTube channel: @LakepointChurch. Video: Mind-blowing Prophecy in the Bible Predicting Islam.

35. Richardson, The Islamic Antichrist, Kindle Format

36. It was around 2024-2025 when I noticed reports in mainstream and

social media about the rise of Islamic influence in Western society. These reports, which included numerous interviews with former Muslims who were now Christian, revealed the growing efforts that were being taken to force radical Islam ideology into the West. As I began to look into this issue I found that many mainstream news articles tended to lean towards "politically correct" findings (perhaps out of fear of Islamic backlash). Yet, former Muslims, like Ayaan Hirsi Ali, and those with 1st hand knowledge of Islam were actually warning the West. I was also reminded of the late Nabeel Qureshi, who converted from Islam to Christianity. He wrote/spoke extensively about his experience with both religions. David Wood of Acts 17 Apologetics also speaks extensively on the teachings of Islam. All of this factored into my writing for this section on Radical Islamist Extremism.

In addition to the sources cited in previous notes, I did find helpful articles from organizations like: Gov.UK "Guidance on the New Definition of Extremism" (2024), csis.org (the Center for Strategic & International Studies) "Islam and the Patterns in Terrorism and Violent Extremism" (2017), Lausanne.org (Lausanne Movement) "What is the Islamic Caliphate and Why Should Christians Care?" (2017).

37. Double Asteroid Redirection Test (DART). NASA Link: https://science.nasa.gov/mission/dart/

    ABCNews.go.com covered the DART test on September 26, 2022. "NASA spacecraft successfully collides with asteroid."

38. News outlets are covering the latest updates on the Artemis II mission program which is scheduled for a lunar landing in 2027. (It is now potentially delayed to 2028). They are also covering updates for the collaboration of various space agencies for the planned mission to Mars around 2030.

39. Greg Bear, September 24, 2013 article: "Don't count 'doomsday asteroid' out yet." Link: https://www.cnn.com/2013/01/23/opinion/bear-apophis-asteroid

40. Sampson, Revelation Now, p.31

Chapter 2: *The Coming Tribulation*

1. Daniel 7:7-27; 8:23-25; 9:27; 11:21-24, 2 Thessalonians 2:3-12; Revelation 13:1-14; 17:1-13

2. Daniel 9:27; 7:19-21; Matthew 24:15-21; 2 Thessalonians 2: 1-4; Revelation 12:1-17; 13:5-7

3. Matthew 24:15-21

4. Isaiah 13:1-13; Joel 2:28-32; Zechariah 14:1-5; Revelation 6:12-17; 19:11-21

5. 2 Thessalonians 2:9-12

6. Many may not be familiar with The Temple Institute's mission to build a 3rd temple in Jerusalem. Their website is: TempleInstitute.org. It is worth examining since Scripture indicates (Daniel 9:27; Matthew 24:15; 2 Thessalonians 2: 1-4; Revelation 11:1-18) that when the Antichrist is in power, he will enter the temple and desecrate the most holy place. For this to happen, a 3rd temple must exist at that time.

7. I have had several conversations with Christians who believe God will forgive them if they take the Mark of the Beast. But they had not read Revelation 13:8,16-17; 14:9-11. These Scriptures are crystal clear. There is no forgiveness for those who take the Mark. A primary reason for this is that in Matthew 12:31-32, Jesus clearly states that blaspheming against the Holy Spirit will never be forgiven.

   In Matthew 26: 63-65, Jesus is on trial and the high priest asks if He is the Son of God. Jesus says "yes" and they accuse Him of blasphemy. What is blasphemy? Declaring yourself to be God when you are not. (Of course Jesus is actually God!) The Antichrist will declare himself to be god and demand global worship. He will commit the ultimate blasphemy against God—which **cannot** be forgiven. Therefore, when a person chooses to take the mark of the Beast, he/she are pledging their allegiance to the Beast and agreeing wholeheartedly with his blasphemy—and will receive the same judgment from God: be cast away into the lake of fire which is the second death (Matthew 25:41,46; Revelation 20:7-15).

8. Dr. John Lennox spoke with Sean McDowell on a YouTube video entitled: "The End of the World? John Lennox on AI and the Book of Revelation"

9. Zuboff, The Age of Surveillance Capitalism: The Fight for a Human Future at the New Frontier of Power, 427, 428

10. RFID Microchip Implants are all the rage within "biohacking" communities and is being used in larger populations at large. Here is a Wikipedia article on the history of the technology, how it's being adopted and its current capabilities.

    Link: https://en.wikipedia.org/wiki/Microchip_implant_(human)#:~:text=RFID implants using NFC technologies,secure element or related technologies

11. Elon Musk's Neural Link website: https://neuralink.com/

12. God is not restricted to only providing blessings in good times. Psalm 23:5 reveals that God can even prepare a table of blessing and provision for us while we are in surrounded by enemies!

13. Kingsnorth, Against the Machine: On the Unmaking of Humanity, 317

Chapter 3: The Greatest Opportunity

1. There were several titles used to refer to Jesus in the Gospels (the Messiah/Christ, Son of David, Son of God, etc.). While Jesus acknowledges each one, the primary title He used for Himself was: "Son of Man." It was commonly thought by modern readers that Jesus' usage of the term, "Son of Man" was the same as how God used the term when addressing the prophet Ezekiel—essentially

calling Ezekiel "human being/mortal." So, it was thought that Jesus was saying to humanity: "I'm human like you." However, thorough research reveals this was not what Jesus meant at all.

In Ezekiel's case, the usage of "Son of Man" is in Hebrew (rendered *"ben-adam"*). However, when Jesus uses the term, He is speaking Aramaic (rendered *"bar 'enash"*). The only other place in Scripture where the term "Son of Man" is written in Aramaic is Daniel chapter 7:13. While it does mean, "human being," when read in context of verses 13 to the end of the chapter, it is undeniable that the term has a significant added dimension which renders it as, "Divine Human Being." The "Son of Man" of Daniel 7 is worshipped by earth's inhabitants and receives an eternal kingdom from the Ancient of Days. Both the Ancient of Days and the Son of Man are divine. They can be none other but God the Father and God the Son.

So, when Jesus uses the term, "Son of Man" to refer to Himself (which he does over 70 times), any biblically literate Jew who heard Him would immediately recognize that He is pointing them back to Daniel 7. In essence, over 70 times, Jesus declared openly, "I am THAT Son of Man which you see in Daniel 7. The One who is divine, who is worshipped and who receives an eternal kingdom from My Father in heaven."

In Matthew 26, when Jesus was on trial, He responded to the high priest by saying, *"From now on you will see the Son of Man sitting at the right hand of the Mighty One and coming on the clouds of heaven."* The high priest and everyone else present knew Jesus was connecting Himself directly with Daniel 7:13. This is why they accused Him of blasphemy because by doing so He declared Himself to be God.

So, every time you read through the Gospels and see Jesus refer to Himself as the Son of Man, know that He is declaring Himself to be God and He is saying He will come again to receive the eternal kingdom from His Heavenly Father. (John also references Jesus as the Son of Man in Revelation 1:13).

For more information on this topic, please read the exceptional book,

Son of Man: The Gospel of Daniel 7, by Samuel Whitefield.

2. The 10/40 window is a region of the planet between 10 and 40 degrees North latitude. It stretches from North Africa across the Middle East and East Asia. This rectangular region houses a high concentration of the world's least reached people groups: Muslims, Hindus, Buddhists, and the world's poorest populations. It is an area of great focus for global missions. It contains two-thirds of the world's population, with many having never heard the gospel.

3. This 10/40 window is the area that many Christian ministries (churches and non-governmental organizations) are now focused on reaching by the year 2030. Once this region has been reached, the entire world will have heard the gospel of Jesus Christ. In Matthew 24:14 Jesus states that when the gospel has been preached to the whole world as a testimony to all nations, then the end will come.

4. The Day of the LORD is a series of global events which culminate with Jesus' return to earth to usher in His eternal kingdom. Ref: Matthew 24:14—25:46; Revelation chapters 6-20.

5. John 15:1-8. Matthew 24:25

6. Mark 4:35-41

Chapter 4: *Weathering the Storm*

1. Global Christian persecution statistics can be found at: Open Doors International: opendoors.org

   You can also find stories about persecuted Christians at The Voice of the Martyrs at: Persecution.com

Chapter 5: After the Storm

1. Zechariah 14:1-9; Matthew 24:30-31; 25:31-32; Luke 21:27; 2 Thessalonians 2:8

2. Revelation 19:11-21; 20:1-3

3. Matthew 13:24-43; 25:31-46; Daniel 12:1-3

4. Isaiah 53; 42:6; 49:6; Luke 2:25-32; John 3:16-21; 4:22; Romans 1:16; Revelation 5:5

5. Richardson, When A Jew Rules the World: What the Bible Really Says About Israel in the Plan of God, 237-239

6. Matthew 19:28; Revelation 21:1-5

7. Matthew 25:21,23

8. Isaiah 25:6-9; Matthew 8:11; 22:1-14

9. Isaiah 65:17-25; Daniel 7:25-27; Matthew 25:34; Revelation 21-22

Closing Thoughts

1. Daniel 7:23-25; Revelation 13:5-7

2. 2 Corinthians 2:11; 1 John 4:1-3

3. Matthew 12:25

4. A good book to help prepare us for the eventuality of suffering for Christ is a book from Voice of the Martyrs. It's entitled, When Faith is Forbidden: 40 Days on the Frontlines with Persecuted Christians, by Todd Nettleton.

5. If you want to know more about the miracles of the Bible and modern-day miracles check out the following:

   Miracles: The Credibility of the New Testament Accounts, by Craig S. Keener (2 Volumes)

   Testing Prayer: Science and Healing, by Candy Gunther Brown

   Watch the series, Miracle, on the Angel App.

6. CBN News reports many Muslims in the Middle East and other parts of the world are coming to faith in Jesus. In many cases, Jesus is appearing to them in dreams and then leading them to Christians who will share the gospel. Links can be found on their YouTube channel. Two such videos are called:
   1) "Dreams and Visions: Muslims Miraculously Coming to Jesus in Dreams" and 2) "Iran's Jesus Revolution? Mosques close as 1 Million Muslims Accept Christ"

7. The anonymous internal poll in Iran was reported by CBN News.

8. Pastor Jack Hibbs, of Calvary Chapel Chino Hills, gave an intriguing teaching on Wednesday February 25, 2026. It was three days before the United States and Israel struck Iran. In this Bible study, he unpacks a prophecy from Jeremiah 49, which relates to Iran and has yet to be fulfilled. This teaching provides a lot of context for understanding what is currently taking place with Iran and the Middle East. The Bible study teaching is on the Youtube channel: Real Life with Jack Hibbs. The name of the study is: "The Stage is Being Set for the End Times!"

9. John 10:10

10. Matthew 5:13-16

11. Romans 5:6-8

APPENDIX

Here are four additional articles which are important for us to consider. I decided not to include them in the body of the book in order to maintain the flow of chapters. Followed by the articles are a listing of various End Times Scriptures in a puzzle format, and a list of books I referenced in this work.

*How Do We Know We Are in the End Times?

*The Great Delusion: Aliens, AI & the Antichrist

*Where is America in the End Times?

*Understanding the Rapture

*End Times Puzzle

*For Further Reading

HOW DO WE KNOW WE ARE IN THE END TIMES?

I am often asked, "When did the Last Days begin? How do we know we are in the End Times?" The Last Days began when Jesus ascended back to heaven. If you look at Acts 1:11, the two angels told the disciples that Jesus would return in the same manner that He just left. So, the "Last Days Clock" began to count down at that moment. Confirmation of this came on the Day of Pentecost when the Holy Spirit was given to the 120 in the upper room. In Acts 2:16-21, Peter quotes from Joel 2 about how **in the last days** the Holy Spirit would be poured out upon believers. In 1 John 2:18, the apostle John states that "it is the last hour..." and that "the antichrist is coming..." So, time is moving.

Here we are, just under 2000 years later. We are closer to Jesus' return than back then. Jesus also gave us another indicator to know when we reached the End Times (which is the latter part of the last days). The indicator is the nation of Israel. In Matthew 24:32-35, Jesus tells us to watch the fig tree (Israel). He indicates at the beginning of that chapter that Israel will fall. This took place in A.D. 70 when Rome destroyed the Jewish temple and then began scattering the Jews to the nations. Jesus then lists numerous signs that will happen leading up to His 2nd Coming. He then says that the generation which sees all of the signs He lists will be the generation to witness His return. To let us know when that generation is, He ties it to the resurrection of the nation of Israel (fig tree).

When we see the nation of Israel come back together, we know we are very close to Christ's 2nd Coming. On May 14, 1948, after almost 1900 years of being exiled to the nations of the world, and after facing a genocide at the hands of Hitler's Nazis during WW2, the Jewish nation was reborn! This was the fulfillment of Jesus' words in Matthew 24, God's prophecy of the valley of dry bones in the first half of Ezekiel 37, and the prophecy in Hosea 6:1-2. Nowhere, at any time in history have we heard of a people that were driven out of their homeland and scattered to the nations of the world for almost 2000 years, coming back to their homeland and being reconstituted as a nation once more! This has been the case for Israel and the Jews—against all odds of human opposition. There is no other way to explain this except that God declared it long ago and so it ***must*** be. God still has a plan for the nation of Israel. One key aspect is to be an indicator of "what time it is" on God's End Times stopwatch.

We are the generation that has seen the nation of Israel return. We are also seeing almost all of the signs Jesus stated—in Matthew 24, Mark 13, Luke 17:20-37; Luke 21—happening within the same timeframe. This is how we can know that we are in the End Times and time is quickly winding up.

Having said all of this, let me also mention that Ezekiel's prophecy comes in two parts. 1) God revives Israel from humanly impossible odds of certain death—bringing the Jews from all over the nations of the world back to their homeland. 2) God makes the Jews spiritually alive as a nation that will be a beacon of light to the rest of the world when God comes to finally dwell with them forever.

The first part of this prophecy has already happened. The nation of Israel exists once again. It also does major work in a variety of international sectors that affects many aspects of the world. Is the nation perfect? No—no nation is! But Israel serves as a mirror in which we can all see ourselves—how we miss the mark... how we need God.

The second part of the prophecy is that Israel will have: a national spiritual renewal. This has not happened yet. It is still future. While there is a growing number of Jews who are coming to faith in Jesus, the nation as a whole has not. On the whole, the nation is still living in unbelief—just like the rest of the world. This is a primary purpose for the Tribulation—which the Bible calls, "the time of Jacob's trouble."

As bad as the Holocaust was, according to Scripture, another will happen at the hands of the Antichrist—which will be worse.

However, it will be through Divine Intervention during this time of great persecution that Israel will see her Rescuer—The One she has pierced—JESUS—and come to know her God in Spirit and in Truth!

So, how do we know we are in the End Times? The signs of the times which Jesus said would happen, are happening. Israel is a nation once more. We are experiencing global-level cataclysmic events. The gospel of the Kingdom is close to being preached to the entire world as a testimony to the nations. And then the end of this age will come.

I believe humanity doesn't have thousands of years left before Jesus returns. I don't think we have hundreds of years left either. We could be looking at decades or less. Time will tell. However, what I do know with 100% certainty, is that even if Jesus' world-wide return is still years away, His return for individual believers happens every day at the moment of our death. So, either way, we need to be ready to meet Him. After all, Jesus told us in John 14:1-3:

1 *"Do not let your hearts be troubled. You believe in God; believe also in me.*
2 *My Father's house has many rooms; if that were not so, would I have told you that I am going there to prepare a place for you?* **3** *And if I go and prepare a place for you, I will come back and take you to be with me that you also may be where I am."*

We **are** in the end times.
Jesus **is** coming soon.
Sooner than we think.
Come Lord Jesus. Come.
Maranatha.

THE GREAT DELUSION:

Aliens, AI and the Antichrist

In chapter one, under the section on deception and the occult, I mentioned extraterrestrials being used as part of the enemy's program to distract us away from truth. I did not have the space in that section to unpack the statement. So, I decided to address it here in this article, which seeks to connect the dots between aliens, artificial intelligence and the antichrist. My purpose is to form a thesis on how the narrative of the great delusion might come together based on current global trends.

The Bible states in 2 Thessalonians 2:9-12 that before Christ returns, God will give the world over to a great delusion. Why? Because people will no longer want truth. They would rather rebel against God and create their own reality.

What happens when you deny God's existence? You replace it with a different set of beliefs. If there is no God who created the universe, then you and I must create our own worldview about how we got here and where we are going. Let me highlight two of the most prevalent worldviews of our generation. Then, I will state what I believe to be their natural conclusion according to the Bible. Much can be said that is beyond the scope of this article. As it stands, this serves as a springboard to help you take serious thought about these two ideologies which are steadily gaining ground in our modern, technologically driven, information-age global society.

IF THERE IS NO GOD...

How did we get here if there is no God? By chance? The more scientists study the properties of the universe and the sheer number of exact specifications that make our life on earth possible, the more the astronomical statistics point to the obvious conclusion. Blind chance and unguided processes could not have made "us", let alone the almost one trillion other lifeforms on this planet. Somewhere, there is a mind behind all of this. But, what mind?

This brings us to the first worldview: a growing number of people believe aliens are responsible for our existence. Some call this the Ancient Astronaut Theory. It posits: at some point in the distant past, an advanced extra-terrestrial species arrived on earth and started (or at least jump-started) all life on this planet. According to those who hold this belief, historical records show that most ancient civilizations share similar stories of "the gods" coming down to earth from the skies. These beings provided vast amounts of information about the stars and planets and helped humans set up civilization. Our ancient ancestors worshiped them and worked for them. Then at some point, the gods left, promising to return. Those who hold to the Ancient Astronaut Theory believe these "gods" were actually aliens from other planets, galaxies and even dimensions.

Given the increasing phenomenon of global UFO and UAP sightings, and the fact that governments are becoming more forthcoming with previously classified information on this subject, it would seem that these beings—if they exist—might in fact be preparing to return. If, one day in the near future, aliens do arrive, how will that change the course of human history? What will that do to our understanding of science, religion and our place in the universe? An even more important question is: If "aliens" do appear, are they really extra-terrestrials from another planet or something more sinister with deceptive motives? Could they be demonic in nature—like the fallen sons of God (angelic beings) we see in Genesis 6, and in the extra-biblical book of 1 Enoch? These beings were known as Watchers. Or could the "aliens" be part of an elaborate human-made deception?

Whichever it may turn out to be, over 61% of the world population from 24 countries believe in the existence of intelligent life from other planets. Also, with all of the movies and television shows on aliens that we are constantly bombarded with, it would seem that humanity is being primed to accept this future possibility.

CAN WE CREATE GOD?

Without a belief in God, the next best thing would be to create our own "god." This is where Artificial Intelligence (AI) enters the picture. Many of the creators of such systems have a 2-part goal in mind. ONE: to give AI access to the totality of all human knowledge so that it can provide solutions to humanity's ills (disease, poverty, war, etc.) and answer life's most existential questions: Who are we as a species? What is our place in the universe? TWO: to use AI to enhance and upgrade human existence to god-like levels by merging humanity with machines (Transhumanism).

Imagine a world where you have 24/7 direct access to an entity that knows the full breath of all human knowledge, is virtually everywhere at the same time and can be seen, heard and touched. You can talk with this entity and receive real-time answers and direction. What would you call it? It's *already* being called a "digital god." According to those on the frontlines of AI development, from Ray Kurzweil to Mo Gawdat, Elon Musk, Sam Altman (and **many others**), this digital reality is almost upon humanity.

Imagine a world where you don't have to die… where, if AI can't cure or repair your decaying body, it could have your consciousness copied and uploaded into a synthetic body or system where you would essentially live forever! *Digital resurrection…* Now, imagine someone willingly choosing this digital immortality even though they don't have a terminal illness.

Even if you are not imagining these scenarios, tech billionaires all over the world, who have vast amounts of resources, are imagining them for you. This is the stuff of science fiction that is now rapidly moving towards becoming science fact. Artificial Intelligence lies at the heart of this pursuit. But sadly, there is a question these developers don't want to honestly confront: What happens to *the soul* of the person who is digitally copied and uploaded?

What a grand deception that would be! A lie straight from the pit of hell. Imagine that a person uploads his or her consciousness to the cloud, with the expectation to live forever in an infinite digital realm, only to discover the horrific reality that their soul (their true self) was never uploaded at all… While the "copy" goes on digitally, the original now stands in hell awaiting the final judgment day of God.

WHERE ARE WE HEADED?

If we have removed God from our worldview and replaced Him with Ancient Astronaut Theory and Transhumanist ideology, where is all of this leading us? It can only lead to one place… or should I say to one person: The Antichrist. Humanity was created with an innate need to worship. And if we will not worship our Creator—GOD—then we will replace Him with an inadequate substitute.

This is what we see in the Bible: a rejection of God's truth in favor of our own lies. God will give us over to our lies. And then one will arrive on the stage of human history who will seem to be the realization of our Alien and AI dreams. This person will bring solutions to our most dire issues, answer our deepest questions, and initiate sweeping change to the planet while promising us godhood.

All this person will require from us in exchange for his blessings will be our worship. We will herald him as our savior, but inwardly he will be our demise. Because if there is a God, as the Bible declares Him to be, then there is also a devil… as the Bible declares *him* to be. And just as God came to earth in the form of Jesus, so the devil will have his counterfeit in the form of the Antichrist—the one who seeks to *replace* Christ.

And what will be his endgame? The Bible tells us this too… the Antichrist wants to deceive as many people as possible ***away*** from the truth of God. He wants to drag as many people as possible ***with him*** to hell: the realm of eternal flames created by God as the place of everlasting punishment for the devil and his angels (Matthew 25:41). In other words, "misery loves company." The creator of misery himself—the devil—wants as much company as possible with him in the lake of fire (which Revelation 20:10-15 calls the second death).

CONCLUSION

Aliens. Artificial Intelligence. The Antichrist. Perhaps you are already alarmed by what you just read. While it is surely concerning, it is not the end of the story. There is so much more that could be said.

While the Bible is clear that a great delusion is coming to the world. It is also clear, that at some point Jesus Christ will return to make everything right! He is the ultimate hope for humanity. Not aliens… Not artificial intelligence… Most certainly not the antichrist! No matter what these three possibilities may promise, what truly matters is the promise made to us by the One who created the universe.

Jesus promises that all who place their faith in Him for their salvation, all who believe that He is the Son of God; that He died on the cross for the forgiveness of our sins; that He rose from the dead on the third day so that death won't have the last word on us: that He ascended back to heaven to prepare a place for us and that He will return to earth again… All who believe in HIM will ***live with Him*** in His eternal Kingdom!

So, if aliens arrive on earth one day saying they are humanity's creators… Or a major breakthrough in artificial intelligence promises us digital godhood... Or a man rises onto the world stage and brings peace to the middle east while demanding global worship… **Do not believe them!** If we are lovers of God and His truth—*with all our heart, mind, soul and strength*—we will not be deceived by the great delusion.

WHERE IS AMERICA IN THE END TIMES?

Many people ask about America's status in the End Times. Because of our nation's cutting-edge technology and military dominance, many believe America must have a central role to play. America is currently a major supporter of Israel, but will that always remain the case?

The prophet Zechariah, speaking on God's behalf, states that there will be a future time when all nations will come against Israel. Here is what it says in Zechariah 12:1-3

1 *"A prophecy: The word of the Lord concerning Israel. The Lord, who stretches out the heavens, who lays the foundation of the earth, and who forms the human spirit within a person, declares:* **2** *"I am going to make Jerusalem a cup that sends all the surrounding peoples reeling. Judah will be besieged as well as Jerusalem.* **3** *On that day, when all the nations of the earth are gathered against her, I will make Jerusalem an immovable rock for all the nations. All who try to move it will injure themselves."*

<u>All the nations of the earth are gathered against Israel</u>.

We each have our own political position and view about Israel's response to the Hamas attack on October 7, 2023. No matter what side of the issue you are on, I believe we can agree on this observation: since then, antisemitism has increased significantly among the nations of the world. The groundwork for the fulfillment of Zechariah's prophecy is being laid. If you read chapters 13 and 14, the prophet lays out the major strokes of what the future global attack on Israel will look like. It will be so devastating that only the LORD will be able to deliver the nation of Israel.

What does this mean for the United States? Where will the country be as the day of Jesus' return becomes imminent? As stated in this book, the nations of the world will eventually unite under a global government during the Tribulation. That world government will ultimately come under the leadership of the Antichrist. The Antichrist will focus on destroying Jews and Christians (and anyone else who refuses to worship him). That means the military armaments of the world will be drawn against Israel. So, if "all the nations of the earth" will be gathered against Israel during that time, then the United States will no longer exist in its present form. Either America will not remain as an ally of Israel, or the nation will no longer be a superpower—and will be too weak to support Israel.

Here are four possible ways this may come about:

ONE: America self-destructs from its own internal strife.

TWO: Enemy nations (or natural disasters) cripple America so it no longer has global military dominance.

THREE: Enemy nations completely destroy America.

FOUR: America is absorbed into the global world government.

All of these possibilities are very sobering to consider.

Where does this leave us today? I thank God for the United States. Even with all of its issues, it has been one of the greatest nations in our modern time. Yes, we should stand and work for the blessing of the nation, like God told the Jews to do when they were held in Babylonian captivity (Jeremiah 29:4-7). But we must realize that only God is God.

The prophet Jeremiah did not like the idea of Israel being taken into captivity. But he submitted himself to God's sovereignty and spoke God's warning to the people so they could be prepared. We face a similar situation. It would seem the handwriting is on the wall. Many believe America will go on indefinitely; meanwhile bad actors are trying to destroy the country from without and within. Therefore, our complete and total allegiance must be placed in Christ alone, because the U.S. government cannot save us from the coming global storm.

Only Jesus can secure our eternal future. This is the lesson God will teach Israel and the world during the Tribulation. The nations must know that God alone is sovereign. Only Christ has the power to truly and completely save an individual, a people and the world.

So, pray that God's will for America and the world will be done. Pray for the salvation of unbelievers and for the saints to be faithful witnesses unto Jesus. No matter what, keep your eyes on Christ! Be "salt and light" to those you meet every day, so they may see your good works and glorify your Father in heaven (Matthew 5:13-16). Praise God for America, but know that we who belong to Jesus are citizens of a heavenly kingdom. Seek the good of the nation for as long as possible, but always live for the glory of God's kingdom.

UNDERSTANDING THE RAPTURE

When will Jesus rapture His Church? Before I answer this question, I need to highlight three things:

ONE: The purpose of the rapture is so the Body of Christ can finally be with Christ. We see this referenced by Jesus in John 14:1-3. Here's what He says:

"Do not let your hearts be troubled. You believe in God; believe also in me. My Father's house has many rooms; if that were not so, would I have told you that I am going there to prepare a place for you? And if I go and prepare a place for you, I will come back and take you to be with me that you also may be where I am."

Jesus goes back to His Father's house (Heaven) to prepare a place for each of us who believe and trust in Him. Why? Because He wants us to be where He is!

TWO: We are currently being "raptured" one at a time. When Jesus completes "our room" our reservation in Heaven is ready. He then calls us home (we die). So, we always need to be ready to meet Jesus because we don't know our death date.

THREE: The ultimate family reunion is coming! The start date, location and time of a family reunion is usually set far in advance. Family members leave from different locations to get to the reunion. They arrive at different times. Some come a week early. Others a day or two early. Some the day of the reunion. All who arrive early fellowship together, but the real festivities don't begin until the official start time. God's Kingdom is similar. God the Father has set the exact time, date and location for His family reunion. The rapture is how we arrive—one at a time and one day as a large group.

FOUR RAPTURE VIEWS

There are 4 views on the timing of the rapture. Three are mainstream and the fourth is lesser known: *Pre-Tribulation. Mid-Tribulation. Post-Tribulation.* And *Pre-Wrath Tribulation. (I define these below.)* Different Christian groups make their case for each. But we must consider an important observation: <u>They can't all be correct</u>. One of them has to be right. The question is, which one?

Unfortunately, talking about the timing of the rapture has caused much division within the church. Some have even said, *"if you don't believe my position on the rapture then you aren't saved."* This mentality is not supported in Scripture. What we need for salvation is one thing: to follow Jesus by placing our belief, faith and trust in Him. The equation for receiving salvation is not having faith in "Jesus + A specific rapture view." It is having faith in "Jesus alone." What we believe about the timing of the rapture is not a "salvation issue," but a "preparation issue." If the Bible reveals the truth on it, then we should want to know so we can better prepare ourselves for the future.

You should know, there is not a single verse in the Bible which states that the rapture of the Church happens <u>*before*</u> the 7-year Tribulation. This belief comes primarily from an *interpretation* of three Scriptures:

1 Thessalonians 5:9 *"For God did not appoint us to suffer wrath but to receive salvation through our Lord Jesus Christ."*

Revelation 3:10 *"Since you have kept my command to endure patiently, I will also keep you from the hour of trial that is going to come on the whole world to test the inhabitants of the earth."*

Luke 21:36 *"Be always on the watch, and pray that you may be able to escape all that is about to happen, and that you may be able to stand before the Son of Man."*

God will keep us from His wrath... Historically, God allows His people to face enemy persecution. But when God pours out His wrath upon a population, He always preserves His people first. 3 biblical examples are: God preserved Noah's family during the flood; God preserved Lot's family before destroying Sodom and Gomorrah; God preserved the Israelites during the 10 plagues on Egypt. So, God does keep His people from experiencing His wrath on unbelievers. Also, the above Scriptures talk about a specific timeframe when God's wrath will come: at the time of Jesus' second coming.

Proponents of a Pre-Tribulation rapture have been taught that the **entire** 7-year tribulation is God's wrath being poured upon the world. If that is true, then we can rightly assume the rapture would happen before the tribulation begins. However, the critical question is this: <u>is the entire 7-years the outpouring of God's wrath</u>?

Proponents of the Mid-Tribulation view believe the **second half** of the 7 Year Tribulation is when God pours out His wrath. Therefore, we must go through the first half (3.5 years), but will be rescued by Jesus at the midpoint just before the Antichrist enters the holy of holies in the 3rd Jewish temple and commits the "abomination which causes desolation." After that moment, all hell literally breaks loose on the earth.

The proponents of the Post-Tribulation view maintain that God will preserve His people **through the entire** Tribulation—much like He preserved the Israelites throughout the entire ten plagues in Egypt.

Again, cases can be made for each option, but they can't all be correct. I encourage you to study them for yourself. Don't just take someone's word. Let your conclusion be based on prayerful consideration of the Scriptural evidence.

WHAT DO I BELIEVE?

People often ask which view I believe. Since I was young, I believed what I was taught: the Pre-Tribulation view. I never seriously considered the other options. However, once I started studying the End Times in 2018, my view began to change. I discovered, as I already shared, that there is not a single Scripture which plainly states the rapture will happen before the Tribulation begins. I was shocked!

After more study, I felt out of the three options (Pre, Mid, Post) the pre-Tribulation viewpoint was the least supported by Scripture. So, I began to lean towards the other two… unsure of which it might be.

While reading Matthew 24 and Revelation 6-8, I saw a clear indication that God's wrath happened during the latter half of the Tribulation. Take a look at the plain reading of Revelation 6-8, which I will summarize. (Please read it for yourself). Jesus opens the 7 seals of the scroll in sequential order, so we can expect the events of each seal to follow the same order as well. Here is what Scripture teaches us.

JESUS OPENS THE 7 SEALS FROM HEAVEN

The opening of the first seal allows the rider on the white horse to be released on the earth. The opening of the second seal allows the rider on the red horse to be released on the earth. The opening of the third seal allows the rider on the black horse to be released on the earth. The opening of the fourth seal allows the rider on the pale horse to be released on the earth. It is believed the rider on the white horse is the Antichrist. What follows is: he takes over the planet through *diplomacy, war, famine and death.*

When Jesus opens the fifth seal, the saints are allowed to be martyred at the hands of the Antichrist and his forces. (Daniel 7:25 and Revelation 13:7 state the Antichrist will wage war against the saints and prevail for a short time.) (AKA: the Great Tribulation.)

However, when Jesus opens the sixth seal, everything begins to shift. A global-level earthquake hits the earth and changes the entire topography of the planet. This strikes immense fear in the population. People run for caves and mountains to hide because they realize God's wrath is about to be poured out upon the earth.

Two events happen next (still within the sixth seal): ***Angels seal the foreheads of the 144,000*** (Revelation 7 &14 says they are celibate men from the 12 tribes of Israel). God preserves them in preparation for the wrath He will pour out on the world. ***Then a scene of celebration happens in heaven!*** An untold multitude of saints from every people group on the planet stand around God's throne praising and worshiping Jesus! *This is clearly the Church. And they have just come out of the Great Tribulation.*

Chapter 8 begins with Jesus opening the seventh and final seal. Heaven falls silent as the time for God's wrath has finally come. It is poured out on an unbelieving world through a series of trumpet and bowl judgments.

CLEAR AS DAY

More could be said, but I think the point is clear. If the outpouring of God's wrath (the Day of the LORD) begins when Jesus opens the 7th seal, then Scripture reveals the rapture happens at some point during the events of the sixth seal!

Jesus says His 2nd coming will be like the days of Lot and Noah *(Luke 17)*. The angels removed Lot's family from the city before it was destroyed (same day). Noah's family and the animals were secured on the Ark the same day the flood began. They were preserved through the entire flood while the rest of humanity and animals perished. The last two major events of the 6th seal are similar. God seals the 144,000 to preserve them while in the midst of the Day of the LORD. God raptures His Church to heaven, removing them prior to the destruction caused by the outpouring of His wrath.

This is the plain reading of the text. I believe it shows the timing of the rapture to be "Pre-Wrath." The Church will go through over half of the Tribulation. God will allow us to face persecution at the hands of the Antichrist system. *(Historically, onlookers have been saved after witnessing God's people boldly facing persecution and death for Jesus. This time will be no different.)* Then, at God's pre-ordained time, He will preserve a remnant of the Jews, rapture His Church and pour out His wrath on the world. For the last 1-2 years of the Great Tribulation, God will use the 144,000 as witnesses to the Jews and the world. Meanwhile the Church will be in heaven experiencing at least three things: 1) The marriage feast (Rev 19). 2) The Bema seat of Christ to receive our rewards (2 Cor 5:10). 3) Preparing to return to earth with Jesus and His angels (Rev 19:14).

CONCLUSION

I love the idea of a Pre-Tribulation rapture! But, if it is incorrect we risk being mentally, physically and spiritually unprepared for the Tribulation. I'd rather be prepared and not need something, than need something and not be prepared. If the Pre-tribulation view proves correct, then we've lost nothing by being prepared to endure. But I believe the Scriptures point to a Pre-Wrath timing.

You may agree or disagree with my conclusion, but keep studying, discussing and praying about it. Try not to let fellow believers divide over it. As followers of Jesus let's seek to understand what Scripture actually teaches, and be willing to jettison our preferred opinions if we find them to be incorrect. Again, getting the rapture timing right is a "preparation issue," not a "salvation issue." The most important thing is that we keep our eyes on Jesus and be ready to meet Him, whether at our death or when the trumpet sounds. This way, we won't fall away from the faith. May we remember that God is faithful to hold and sustain us through any and every trial! Whenever Jesus comes... I want to be ready to see Him face-to-face. I pray you do too.

PUTTING THE PIECES TOGETHER

The following passages --when taken together-- will provide a clear framework on the End Times and the Return of Christ. Please study entire chapters for context.

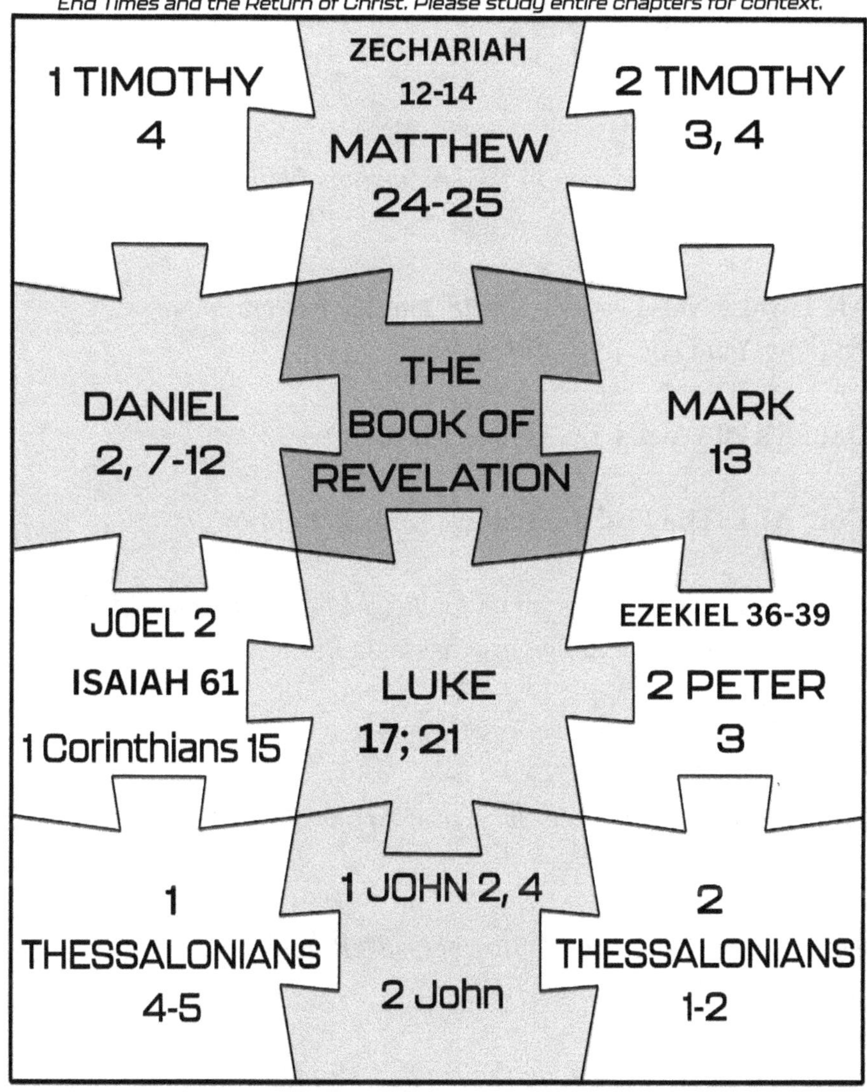

FOR FURTHER READING

—**Against the Machine:** *On the Unmaking of Humanity,* Paul Kingsnorth

—**All Things New:** *Heaven, Earth, and the Restoration of Everything You Love,* John Eldredge

—**Daniel's 70 Weeks**, Dr. Chuck Missler

—**God, AI & The End of History**, John C. Lennox

—**god of A.I.:** *The Deification of Artificial Intelligence and the Rise of a New Technomancy Religion,* Anastasia Bar

—**Homo Deus:** *A Brief History of Tomorrow,* Yuval Noah Harari

—**Life 3.0:** *Being Human in the Age of Artificial Intelligence,* Max Tegmark

—**Resurrection:** *The BIG Picture of God's Purpose and Your Destiny,* Allen Paul Weaver III

—**Revelation Now:** *Viewing the Tragedies and Triumph of Believers: Building Faith Now,* Shellie Sampson, Jr.

—**Revelation and the End Times:** *Unraveling God's Message of Hope,* Ben Witherington III

—**The Age of Surveillance Capitalism:** *The Fight for a Human Future at the New Frontier of Power,* Shoshana Zuboff

—**The Islamic Antichrist:** *The Shocking Truth about the Real Nature of the Beast,* Joel Richardson

—**The Pre-Wrath Rapture of the Church:** *A New Understanding of the Rapture, the Tribulation, and the Second Coming,* Marvin Rosenthal

—**The Dragon's Prophecy:** *Israel, the Dark Resurrection, and the End of Days,* Jonathan Cahn

—**When Faith is Forbidden:** *40 Days on the Frontlines with Persecuted Christians,* Todd Nettleton

—**When A Jew Rules the World:** *What the Bible Really Says About Israel in the Plan of God,* Joel Richardson

ACKNOWLEDGMENTS

I want to thank my wife, Ijnanya for being a constant support on this journey to study and understand the events surrounding Jesus' 2nd Coming. Thank you for all of the late-night, early-morning, and mid-day conversations and prayers about this book! I also want to say, "thank you" for believing in me as a writer and preacher of the gospel of God's kingdom. I am truly grateful the LORD brought us together all of those years ago...

I want to say, "thank you" to my son, Noble. You didn't ask to have a father as a preacher. But that is what God determined when He told your mother and I to have you. Because of your proximity, you've learned about the End Times—even as I tried to keep you shielded from some of the subject's fearful elements. You've raised many great questions and shared your own insights. Both have helped to shape my own study and understanding. Know that I am proud of you!

I would like to also thank Deon Allen, Janice Francis, Tanya Thurman and Duane Roquemore for reading portions of the early draft of this book. Your feedback and encouragement has been very helpful.

Finally, I want to thank every sister and brother in Christ—from 2018 to today—who participated in my teachings on the End Times: from Sunday congregations, to Wednesday Bible studies, to day-sessions and week-long workshops, conferences and virtual classes... Thank you for all of your questions, comments and encouragement as you sought to understand the Scriptures in light of where we are in human history. May we all seek to be ready to meet Jesus when He comes... and may we help others do the same.

ABOUT THE AUTHOR

Rev. Allen Paul Weaver III is an ordained preacher and teacher, who has served in ministry for over 30 years. He has authored 10 previous books, blog posts and articles geared around Christian living, personal development and the End Times.

Rev. Allen helps believers to: 1) Grow in their relationship with Jesus. 2) Discover, develop and deploy their gifts for God's glory. 3) Prepare for Jesus' Return (either at the point of their death or when He parts the sky and every eye will see Him).

Rev. Allen is married. He and his wife have one son. Find out more about him at: www. AllenPaulWeaver3.com.

Other books by Rev. Allen

Autobiographical
Transition: Breaking Through the Barriers

Young Adult Fiction
Speedsuit Powers: Book 1—The Prototype
Speedsuit Powers: Book 2—The Opposition
Speedsuit Powers: Book 3—The Revelation
Flight: A Speedsuit Powers Story
Discourse: A Speedsuit Powers Story

Supernatural Fiction
Sovereign

Personal Development
MOVE! Your Destiny is Waiting on You

Christian Living & The End Times
Resurrection: The BIG Picture of God's Purpose & Your Destiny
The Resurrection Life: A 40 Day Journey with Jesus

www.ingramcontent.com/pod-product-compliance
Lightning Source LLC
LaVergne TN
LVHW020640100826
845148LV00012B/2261

9781736097274